CHRIST OUR SUFFICIENCY

CHRIST
OUR SUFFICIENCY

by

EVANGELIST OLIVER B. GREENE

The Gospel Hour, Inc., Oliver B. Greene, Director
P. O. Box 2024
Greenville, South Carolina

CONTENTS

CONTENT

CHRIST OUR SAVIOUR

CHRIST OUR SAVIOUR

AND SHE SHALL BRING FORTH A SON, AND THOU SHALT CALL His name JESUS: for He shall save His people from their sins" (Matt. 1:21).

We read in the Word of God concerning "the Son of God . . . the Son of man . . . the Christ of God . . . the man Christ Jesus . . ." and all of these titles refer to one and the same Person; but we cannot *appreciate* Jesus as the Son of God and at the same time the Son of man until we know Him as our personal Saviour. We will not be able to understand *Jesus, Saviour of sinners,* until we know Him personally through the marvelous grace of God.

It is true that centuries before the Saviour was born, it was prophesied that *He would be born* (Isa. 9:6, 7), and that He would be born of a virgin (Isa. 7:14). His royal lineage and His miraculous conception were prophesied, but it is outstanding and singular that the first *announcement* concerning the birth of Jesus has to do with His *character* as Saviour of sinners.

9

After the salutation and introduction of his letter to the Romans, Paul sets forth the total depravity of man, then declares that the Gospel is the power of God unto salvation to all who believe — to the Jew first, and then to the Gentile; and immediately following the declaration of the condition of fallen man, Paul declares that *the blood of Jesus Christ* is sufficient to save whosoever will believe:

". . . There is no difference: for all have sinned, and come short of the glory of God; being justified freely by His grace through the redemption that is in Christ Jesus: whom God set forth to be a propitiation through faith in His blood to declare His righteousness for the remission of sins that are past, through the forbearance of God; to declare, I say, at this time, His righteousness: that He might be just, and the justifier of him which believeth in Jesus" (Rom. 3:22-26).

HIS PERSON - HIS WORK

In considering the Lord Jesus Christ as Saviour of sinners, two things must be pointed out: First, His person. Second, His work.

1. *His Person*:

There is the action of God the Father in raising Jesus the Son from the dead and placing Him at His own right hand in the heavenlies (I Tim. 2:5; Heb. 1:1-3). God raised up Jesus from the dead and, in so doing, testified that Jesus finished the work which He sent Him forth to accomplish; and *because* Jesus completed the work, fulfilling the law and the prophets (Matt. 5:17) and satisfying the law of God (Rom. 8:1-3), in the resurrection and ascension God the Father exhibits and declares that *Jesus the Son is Saviour of sinners because of His finished work.* God the Father has placed His divine stamp of approval upon the life and work of the Son of whom He said, "This is my beloved Son, in whom I am well pleased" (Matt. 17:5).

In considering the Person of Christ, we read in Romans 1:1-4, "Paul, a servant of Jesus Christ, called to be an apostle, separated unto the Gospel of God, (Which He had promised afore by His prophets in the holy Scriptures,) concerning His Son Jesus Christ our Lord, which was made of the seed of David according to the flesh; and declared to be the Son of God with power, according to the spirit of holiness, by the resurrection from the dead."

In Matthew 1:1 we read, "The book of the generation of Jesus Christ, the *son of David,* the *son of Abraham.*"

He is also declared to have been begotten by the Holy Ghost. In Matthew 1:18-25 we learn that Joseph, being a just man and learning that his espoused virgin was with child, was about to put her away when God informed him that Mary was to bring forth the Saviour of sinners, and name Him *JESUS.*

Before we can see Jesus as Saviour of sinners we must see and believe that He was very God in flesh. Before we can accept *what He DID* we must realize *who He was.* If He was not very God in flesh (II Cor. 5:19) then He was the world's greatest imposter! In the eighth chapter of John's Gospel Jesus announced that He and the heavenly Father were one. He declared that He proceeded FROM God the Father and would return TO God the Father. The Jews took up stones to stone Him — but He did not come into the world to be stoned: He came to die on a cross in order that He might become *the Saviour of sinners.*

As a general rule, the sinner looks at the *works* of Jesus before considering *the Person who performs the works.* When Nicodemus came to Jesus, the first words he uttered were, "Rabbi, we know that thou art a teacher come from God: for no man can do these miracles that thou doest, except God be with him" (John 3:2). Nicodemus had been attracted through the *works* of Jesus rather than by His Person. It is true that he confessed that no ordinary man could do what

the Lord was doing; but it was not *the miracles* He was performing daily that could save Nicodemus. It was not the
mighty works He was doing. *It was the death of the man
Christ Jesus and His shed blood that could save from sin.*

The first words of Nicodemus to Jesus pointed out the
mighty works He was doing; but in answering this ruler in
Israel, Jesus declared that He had come down from heaven,
and announced the fact of His rejection and crucifixion:

". . . No man hath ascended up to heaven, but He
that came down from heaven, even the Son of man which
is in heaven. And as Moses lifted up the serpent in the
wilderness, even so must the Son of man be lifted up: That
whosoever believeth in Him should not perish, but have
eternal life" (John 3:13-15). Nicodemus was a master in
the religion of the Jews, and he immediately understood the
Lord's reference to the episode in the wilderness when Moses
made the serpent of brass and placed it on a pole as instructed by God.

Jesus was the God-Man: ". . . God was in Christ, reconciling the world unto Himself, not imputing their trespasses
unto them; and hath committed unto us the word of reconciliation" (II Cor. 5:19). Jesus was truly man — He was
flesh; but He was the God-Man — *truly God,* and truly *man.*
He was God manifest in flesh:

"In the beginning was the Word, and the Word was with
God, and the Word was God . . . And the Word was made
flesh, and dwelt among us, (and we beheld His glory, the
glory as of the only begotten of the Father,) full of grace
and truth" (John 1:1 and 14). It is a Bible fact that *the Word
was the Eternal Son.* It is also a Bible fact that *the Eternal
Son became man* — just as truly man as any person who ever
walked upon the face of this earth. *He was God AND man.*

Jesus Christ the Son of God presented a union of extremes
not possible in any other. There has never been — nor will
there ever be — another Jesus. His Person was so unfathom-

able, so incomprehensible, that He Himself declared, ". . . No man knoweth the Son, but the Father . . ." (Matt. 11:27). Man has achieved much; he has made great strides in many fields. We have intellectual giants today, and man is truly working miracles through science and chemistry. But there is one Person who cannot be placed in a test tube or under a microscope and be broken down, divided, or understood through the wisdom and achievements of man. That Person is Jesus — Son of God, yet Son of man; very God in flesh.

The eternal, holy God whom Adam offended was wrapped up in the flesh of *the second Adam* (II Cor. 5:19). Jesus was therefore the offended God, in the flesh of the offender. Unfathomable? Yes! Incomprehensible? Yes! Beyond man's understanding? Yes — but the Saviour of sinners, nevertheless. Millions have testified to His saving grace. Millions live today who have their faith in the finished work and shed blood of the man Christ Jesus — Saviour of sinners. It is imperative that we believe and hold fast both His true divinity (He was God), and His equal nature as man (true humanity). He was human, but He was also divine.

Did I hear someone say, *"I cannot understand that"?* Thank God that you cannot understand it, for if you could, you would be as wise as the God who provided the virgin-born Saviour, JESUS. I am so thankful that the God in whom I trust is wiser and more powerful than I; and although I do not *understand* the incarnation, I believe it. I believe that Jesus was God, yet man. I believe that He took my place and died on the cross for my sins. I have put my faith in His finished work, and therefore I have peace with God. I cannot *explain* the incarnation. I cannot explain *the new birth* — but I can testify that it works in a human heart, because it has worked in my own heart for more than twenty-nine years!

If Jesus had not been truly man, had He not been made of flesh exactly like your flesh and mine (but without our sin), He could not have been a true sacrifice FOR sin. He had to be as we are, and in such a body completely over-come sin and temptation, in order that He might offer Him-self a sacrifice for sin — the purpose for which He came into the world (John 1:29). It is equally true that had Jesus been only *man,* His sacrifice could not have satisfied God, nor could it have made salvation available to "whosoever will."

It took a holy God to provide what a holy God demands — pure righteousness and true holiness: "Follow peace with all men, and holiness, without which no man shall see the Lord" (Heb. 12:14).

The devil knows that Jesus was the God-Man. While Jesus was here on earth, the demons confessed in an audible voice that they knew who He was: "And, behold, they cried out, saying, What have we to do with thee, Jesus, thou Son of God? Art thou come hither to torment us before the time?" (Matt. 8:29).

Actually, the *devil* has more respect for Jesus than a liberal or a modernist has. Liberalism and modernism deny the incarnation and the virgin birth; they contend that Jesus was a great teacher, but they do not teach that He was God in flesh. One group denies the humanity of Jesus, another denies His Divinity. Both groups are in error. They are tools of Satan, used to damn the souls of sinners.

The glory of the Person of Christ lies in the fact that He was both God and man, divine yet human, in one Person. This truth lies at the foundation (and is the heart) of redemption. Had Jesus been just man, His blood could not atone for sin any more than could the blood of any other man. He was man in flesh, but His blood came from God: "Forasmuch then as the children are *partakers* of flesh and blood, He also Himself likewise *took part* of the same; that through death He might destroy him that had the power of death, that is, the devil; and deliver them who through fear of death were all their lifetime subject to bondage" (Heb. 2:14, 15).

"Take heed therefore unto yourselves, and to all the flock,

over the which the Holy Ghost hath made you overseers, to feed the church of God, which He hath purchased *with His own blood*" (Acts 20:28).

Let us follow Jesus from Bethlehem to Calvary: (Read Matthew, Mark, Luke, and John.) As He walked and talked, as He tabernacled among men, we see the unfolding of both the human and the divine. As He walked with His disciples, we see Him hungry, thirsty, tired, resting His weary body at Jacob's well while He waited for the return of His disciples who had gone into the city to buy bread. We see Him standing at the tomb of a friend, weeping with the loved ones who grieved. We find Him sleeping in the hinder part of a ship, while His disciples cry out with fear of the storm. Human? Yes! Divine? Yes! *He spoke, and the dead came forth alive from the tomb. He rebuked the wind and the waves, commanding the storm to cease. The wind stopped blowing, the waves ceased their rolling, and the little ship encountered "a great calm"* (Mark 4:35-39).

Even His own disciples — those who were closest to Him — cried out, *"What manner of man is this, that even the wind and the sea obey Him?"* Please read also Isaiah 52:14, the entire fifty-third chapter of Isaiah, and the eleventh chapter of John.

Jesus was so human — yet the things He did puzzled His disciples and confounded His enemies. He was so human, so humble, so like other men — yet He did things that even His enemies confessed only God could do! They said, "Who but God could cleanse the leper? Who but God could open the eyes of the blind, raise the dead, and control the wind and the waves? Could he who has a demon do these miracles?"

Even Philip demanded proof that Jesus had proceeded from the Father: "Philip saith unto Him, Lord, shew us the Father, and it sufficeth us. Jesus saith unto him, Have I been so long time with you, and yet hast thou not known

me, Philip? He that hath seen me hath seen the Father; and
how sayest thou then, Shew us the Father? Believeth thou
not that I am in the Father, and the Father in me? The words
that I speak unto you I speak not of myself: but the Father
that dwelleth in me, He doeth the works. Believe me that
I am in the Father, and the Father in me: or else believe
me for the very works sake" (John 14:8-11).

Regardless of what liberals, modernists, and even atheists
may say about Jesus, Paul admonishes, ". . . Let God be true,
but every man a liar" (Rom. 3:4). To any honest person
who will read the Bible with an open mind, without pre-
conceived ideas, the Scriptures declare and prove beyond
a shadow of doubt that Jesus was very God, and yet He
was true humanity. "In the beginning was the Word, and
and the Word was with God, and the Word was God. . .
And the Word was made flesh, and dwelt among us. . . No
man hath seen God at any time; the only begotten Son, which
is in the bosom of the Father, He hath declared Him" (John
1:1, 14, and 18).

Paul describes Jesus as "the brightness of God's glory and
the express image of His Person" (Heb. 1:3). In Colossians
1:15-17 we read, "Who is the image of the invisible God, the
firstborn of every creature: For by Him were all things
created, that are in heaven, and that are in earth, visible and
invisible, whether they be thrones, or dominions, or principalities, or powers: All things were created by Him, and for
Him: and He is before all things, and by Him all things
consist."

Jesus proclaimed, in His own emphatic, dogmatic, but
"HE THAT HATH SEEN ME HATH SEEN THE
FATHER" (John 14:9).

"I AND MY FATHER ARE ONE" (John 10:30).

"VERILY, VERILY, I SAY UNTO YOU, BEFORE
ABRAHAM WAS, *I AM*" (John 8:58).

Dear reader, with these clear statements before us, how can anyone doubt that Jesus was very God — *Divine!*

God is an eternal Spirit — from everlasting to everlasting. There was never a time when God was not, there will never be a time when God shall not be. He had no beginning, He will have no ending. It is utterly impossible for the mind of man to begin to comprehend God; but Jesus who was in the bosom of the Father *declared Him.* As we read the Gospel we discover that Jesus was in the beginning with the Father, equal with the Father in glory, omnipotent, omniscient, and omnipresent. The Word which was *in the beginning with God* was made flesh, and Jesus (the Word in flesh) announced and declared the eternal God who so loved us that He planned and perfected our salvation in the Saviour — the Son of His love, the only begotten of the Father.

As we study the Gospel, we read that all things were created by Jesus, and without Him was not anything made that was made. He made the world and all that therein is. He created the heavens and the earth — and yet, *it is NOT His works that save us;* it is His Person, on the cross, dying the death that should have been meted out to every sinner who ever will live on this earth! Christ died in our stead.

The foundation of the earth rests upon Him who was despised and rejected of men, spit upon, nailed to a cross — and the crowds around Him mocked as He died; but *before* the foundation of this earth was laid, it was already settled that Jesus would pay the sin-debt with His own blood (I Pet. 1:18-25).

It is utterly impossible to become a Christian apart from embracing the incarnation and the virgin birth. We must believe that Jesus was the God-Man — truly God, yet truly man — the virgin-born Saviour who lived on earth, was tempted in all points as we are tempted, yet was without sin. He was nailed to a cross, He died, He was buried, and He is risen.

It is a divine imperative that we believe that Jesus was very God in flesh, reconciling the world unto Himself; and if we refuse to believe that, we HAVE no Saviour, we have no salvation, and we are hopelessly doomed to the lake of fire.

2. *His Work*:

If we rely on the finished work of Christ apart from any human effort or human work, we are safe. If we have responded to His Word, we are *sure* that we are safe. Those of us who have *surrendered to His will* are saved, sure, and happy. It is the spiritual birthright of every believer to enjoy "abundant life."

It is not the spotless, sinless *life* of Jesus that saves sinners. It is His death alone, apart from anything else — the fact that He bore the sins of sinners: "Who His own self bare our sins in His own body on the tree, that we, being dead to sins, should live unto righteousness: by whose stripes ye were healed" (I Pet. 2:24).

The spotless, sinless life of Jesus revealed what He was, displaying His divine *qualifications* to be the offering for sin. His spotless life proved Him to be the Lamb of God, because He was the only sinless one who ever lived upon the face of this earth. He was truly the Lamb without spot or blemish, the Lamb that only God could provide. *But it was on the cruel cross of Calvary that He stood in the place where every sinner should stand because of his sins.* On the cross Jesus met all of God's righteous demands. *He* endured the wrath that was due every sinner because of his sin. Jesus, the spotless Lamb of God, took your place and mine, willingly, on the cross. It was there that He bore our sin and paid the sin-debt.

It is the *blood* of Jesus — not His perfect, sinless life — that makes atonement: "For the life of the flesh is in the blood: and I have given it to you upon the altar to make an atonement for your souls: *for it is the blood that maketh an atonement for the soul*" (Lev. 17:11). Please study Leviticus chapters 1, 2, and 16.

Throughout the earthly life of Jesus He was "a man of sorrows, and acquainted with grief"; but as He walked the dusty roads of Judaea and along the shore of the Sea of Galilee, He was ever conscious of His Father's love, and He knew that He was doing His Father's will. Everything He said and did was to God's glory and in His name. No dark shadow ever passed between the soul of Jesus and God the Father; but on the cross God smote the Lamb and dealt with Christ concerning sin (Isa. 53:4).

Jesus testified, "When ye have lifted up the Son of man, then shall ye know that I am he, and that I do nothing of myself; but as my Father hath taught me, I speak these things. And He that sent me is with me: the Father hath not left me alone; for I do always those things that please Him" (John 8:28, 29).

The Son of God did always the things that pleased His heavenly Father and the sunshine of God's love flooded His pathway, even though He was a man of sorrows and acquainted with grief; but when He reached Calvary and was nailed to the cross, everything changed. When the cross was raised between heaven and earth, then and there the spotless Lamb of God was "made sin for us":

"For He (God) hath made Him (Jesus) to be sin for us, who knew no sin; that we might be made the righteousness of God in Him" (II Cor. 5:21). It was then that the unfathomable anguish of His spirit cried out, *"My God, my God! Why hast thou forsaken me?"* (Matt. 27:46).

Dearly beloved, has it ever occurred to you that for the moments on Calvary as He paid the sin-debt, the Son of God absolutely and completely lost sight of the face and the smile of the heavenly Father? He was of necessity forsaken of God, because Jesus voluntarily made Himself a sacrifice for sin:

"Therefore doth my Father love me, because I lay down my life, that I might take it again. No man taketh it from me, but I lay it down of myself. I have power to lay it down, and I have power to take it again. This commandment have I received of my Father" (John 10:17, 18).

At the awful, indescribable moment when the soul of Jesus was made an offering for sin and God was dealing with sin in the Son, it was a divine imperative that the heavenly Father turn His back on the Son, because God is the eternal Father of righteousness and holiness, and that holiness forbade His looking upon sin — even unto His only begotten Son as He paid our sin-debt!

Yes, Jesus satisfied the heart of God, even to the laying down of His spotless, sinless life through death on the cruel cross, that we might be made the righteousness of God in Him. So we see that it was not as He walked this earthly journey, cleansing the lepers, opening the eyes of the blind, healing the sick and raising the dead; but it was on the cruel cross of Calvary, by the shedding of His precious blood, that the atonement was accomplished. Before the Lamb of God, the Saviour of Sinners, bowed His head and gave up the Ghost, He gave forth a cry of victory: "IT IS FINISHED! ! !" (John 19:30).

The finished work of Jesus is so complete, so thoroughly accomplished, and in it God was so glorified, that on the merit and foundation of that finished work a sinless, Holy God is now able to save sinners and still be righteous. He can still be just — and yet justify the ungodly who deserve hell — but only on the merit of the finished work of Jesus. Although God is glorified in the saving of everyone who believes, He saves us only for Jesus' sake: "And be ye kind one to another, tenderhearted, forgiving one another, *even as God for Christ's sake hath forgiven you*" (Eph. 4:32).

In the heavenlies, in the ages to come, God will display the exceeding riches of His grace in Christ Jesus: "But God who is rich in mercy, for His great love wherewith He loved us, even when we were dead in sins, hath quickened us together with Christ . . . and hath raised us up together, and made us sit together in heavenly places in Christ Jesus: *That in the ages to come He might shew the exceeding riches of His grace in His kindness toward us through Christ Jesus*" (Eph. 2:4-7).

Just as all things were created by Him, for Him, and through Him, "and without Him was not anything made that was made, in heaven or in earth," it is also true that all blessings of all believers flow from and are made possible through the finished work of the Lamb of God.   There are blessings that will be enjoyed by all believers in the Millennium — the one thousand years of glorious peace on earth.   There are blessings to be enjoyed in the new heaven, in the new earth, and in the Pearly White City. All the eternal blessings and the happiness of the saints of all ages, the perfecting of the new creation of God, will come to us through the finished work of the Lord Jesus Christ, who laid His life down for sinners that we, enemies of God, hopeless, strengthless, might have a Saviour.

The work of Jesus has two aspects: First, *Toward God;* then, *toward man.* First and foremost, God must be satisfied — the righteous, holy God who could not look upon sin; the God who clearly instructed Adam, "The day you eat thereof, you shall surely die!"

In the Old Testament era under the law, on the great day of atonement the blood of the sin-offering was carried within the holy of holies and sprinkled "upon the mercy-seat eastward; and before the mercy seat shall (the priest) sprinkle of the blood with his finger seven times" (Lev. 16:14).   This act of sprinkling the blood was done with blood of the bullock (which was the offering for Aaron and his house), and also with the blood of the goat of the sin-offering which was for the chosen people, Israel.

What we must see here is the fact that in both instances the blood was *for God*, offered to satisfy His holiness. The blood was sprinkled *before* the mercy seat as well as *upon* it in the holy of holies — sprinkled there seven times — so that when the worshipper drew nigh he might find the perfect testimony, the blood, in the presence of a holy God.

The blood was *for God*, atonement being made with the blood in accordance with the requirements of His holiness and the righteousness of His throne; and the blood made propitiation for the sins of the people.

The Lamb of God, spotless and without blemish, was made the propitiation *for OUR sins*: "And He is the propitiation for our sins: and not for our's only, but also for the sins of the whole world" (I John 2:2).

Thus we see that *the power, the value, and the cleansing* of the blood of Christ is according to its value in the eyes of Almighty God, and that value is INFINITE. Because of its unspeakable preciousness before God the Father (inasmuch as He had been glorified by the blood and at such a cost), it became the foundation on which God is able to deal in grace with the whole world, and to send out His servants — ministers, evangelists, and missionaries — with the glorious message, "Be ye reconciled to God!" (II Cor. 5:19).

"For God so loved the world, that He gave His only begotten Son, that whosoever believeth in Him should not perish, but have everlasting life" (John 3:16).

The other aspect of the work of Jesus on Calvary is *toward man* — the work of substitution, the shadow of which is set forth by "the live goat" as recorded in Leviticus 16:20-22:

"And when he hath made an end of reconciling the holy place, and the tabernacle of the congregation, and the altar, he shall bring the live goat: and Aaron shall lay both his hands upon the head of the live goat, and confess over him all the iniquities of the children of Israel, and all their transgressions in all their sins, putting them upon the head of the goat, and shall send him away by the hand of a fit man INTO THE WILDERNESS: And the goat shall bear upon him all their iniquities INTO A LAND NOT INHABITED: and he shall let go the goat in the wilderness."

In Romans 3:25 we have the same truth set forth concerning Jesus, where He is shown as the "Mercy Seat" through faith in His blood: "*Whom God hath set forth to be a propitiation through faith in His blood, to declare His righteousness for the remission of sins that are past, through the forbearance of God.*" (In the most holy place stood the ark. The mercy seat — a slab of pure gold with a cherub at each end — rested on the ark. The name of this slab, *kapporet,* means "to cover." In the Levitical ritual it meant "propitiatory." Read the account in Exodus 25:10-22; 37:1-8.

In Romans 4:25 we read, "Who was delivered for our offences, and was raised again for our justification."

So we see that not only has propitiation been provided which made it possible for God to be just and justify the sinner through the blood of Jesus, the Lamb without spot or blemish, but believers can say that He, the Lamb, was delivered for our offences, He has borne our sins in His own body on the tree, and has carried our sins away "into a land not inhabited" and left them there, never to be remembered against us any more. Our sins are gone; they can never be found. They are left in a land not inhabited, they are cast into the depths of the sea. God has put our sins behind His back and has forgotten them forever!

Christ was delivered for our offences, He has been raised again for our justification, and we know beyond a shadow of doubt that He lives at the right hand of God the Father, making intercession for all believers. Jesus dealt with sin and SINS in His cross:

"For what the law could not do, in that it was weak through the flesh, God sending His own Son in the likeness of sinful flesh, and for sin, condemned sin in the flesh" (Rom. 8:3).

Not only has God the Father been satisfied and glorified in the shed blood of Jesus, but both the entire need and the state of the sinner are met, thoroughly and completely, in the work of Christ, in His cross. In the cross of the Lord Jesus Christ, the truth of all the sacrifices made under law in the Old Testament is embodied — the burnt offering as well as the sin-offering; the Paschal Lamb as well as the sacrifices on the day of atonement. All these were shadows of the Lamb of God — spotless, sinless, very God in flesh — who came to take away the sin of the world by ONE sacrifice, the sacrifice of Himself, once, for all, forever, never to be repeated.

In I Corinthians 15:1-4 we have the divine definition of the Gospel — the death, burial, and resurrection of Jesus *"according to the Scriptures."* The resurrection of the Son of God has a singular and special significance, for *apart* from the resurrection there is no hope. Apart from the resurrection, all preaching and all faith is empty and vain.

Peter says, "Him, being delivered by the determinate counsel and foreknowledge of God, ye have taken, and by wicked hands have crucified and slain: Whom God hath raised up, having loosed the pains of death: because it was not possible that He should be holden of it" (Acts 2:23, 24).

Again and again throughout the New Testament, the Holy Spirit emphasizes the fact that God raised up Jesus and exalted Him *at His right hand.* Study Acts 3:14, 15; 4:10; 5:30 and 31.

The Apostle Paul also declares that the resurrection is a divine imperative for salvation. Study Acts. 13:27-31; 17:31; Romans 4:24, 25; I Corinthians 15; Ephesians 2.

The greatest bombshell ever to explode in the face of an unbelieving world was the bodily resurrection of Jesus Christ. The empty tomb baffled His enemies. The fact that God raised Him from the dead and seated Him at the right hand of His Majesty expresses God's estimate of the value of the work of Jesus here on earth.

Just before He began His march to Calvary, the Lord Jesus Himself presents this tremendous truth. After Judas had gone out to betray Him, He said, "Now is the Son of man glorified, and God is glorified in Him. If God be glorified in Him, God shall also glorify Him in Himself, and shall straightway glorify Him" (John 13:31, 32).

In His intercessory prayer, recorded in the seventeenth chapter of John, Jesus prayed to the heavenly Father in these words:

"I have glorified thee on the earth: I have finished the work which thou gavest me to do. And now, O Father, glorify thou me with thine own self with the glory which I had with thee before the world was" (John 17:4, 5).

The resurrection (and the fact that Jesus is now seated at the right hand of God the Father) testifies that God is pleased and glorified in His Son who "became obedient unto death, even the death of the cross" (Phil. 2:8-10).

What is the message to believers? Tremendous it is — hear it: *Christ bore our sins in His own body on the cross. He went down into death under the wrath and judgment due US. The fact that God raised Him from the dead proves beyond any shadow of doubt that our sins are gone.*

And where IS our Substitute? Is He in the grave? No! He lives — and He is now seated at the right hand of His Majesty on high (Heb. 1:1-3). The man Christ Jesus is now at the right hand of God the Father, making intercession for us (I. Tim. 2:5). He is not in the tomb — He is in glory; and since He who bore our sins became obedient unto death, even the death of the cross, and is now in the glory seated at the right hand of God, *we know that our sins are gone.*

The fact that there is a Man in heaven — the Man Christ Jesus, and that He is seated at the right hand of God the Father, proves that the sin-question is forever settled, and

God is glorified in the finished work — the death, burial, and resurrection of the Son of His love, the only begotten of God.

Jesus said, "I have glorified thee on earth, I have finished the work which thou gavest me to do." Therefore, God has glorified His Son with Himself and given to Him *the glory He had with the Father* before the world was. The Man, Christ Jesus, now seated at the right hand of God the Father, is the Mediator between God and men. He bore our sins, He took our place, He has been received by the Father and He is our Mediator. He became our scapegoat — He took our sins and bore them away. But now, He who was our scapegoat is seated in glory at the right hand of God the Father, and this fact assures me that since God has accepted our Substitute and given Him the highest seat in heaven, we need have no fear; because Jesus said if we would confess Him before men, He would confess us before the heavenly Father.

HOW ARE WE SAVED?

In the Scripture we have clearly seen that Jesus is the Saviour, the Lamb of God without spot or blemish. He willingly took our place and bore our sins in His own body on the cross. But *how* are we saved? How do we come into possession of salvation? How does the miracle of the new birth become ours? There is only one place to find the right answer, and that is in the Word of God:

John 3:16-18: "For God so loved the world, that He gave His only begotten Son, that whosoever believeth in Him should not perish, but have everlasting life.. For God sent not His Son into the world to condemn the world; but that the world through Him might be saved. He that believeth on Him is not condemned: but he that believeth not is condemned already, because he hath not believed in the name of the only begotten Son of God."

John 3:36: "He that believeth on the Son hath everlasting life: and he that believeth not the Son shall not see life; but the wrath of God abideth on him."

John 6:47: "Verily, verily, I say unto you, He that believeth on me hath everlasting life."

Romans 5:1: "Therefore being justified by faith, we have peace with God through our Lord Jesus Christ."

Ephesians 2:8, 9: "For by grace are ye saved through faith; and that not of yourselves: it is the gift of God: Not of works, lest any man should boast."

To the wicked jailer in Philippi, Paul and Silas said, "Believe on the Lord Jesus Christ, and thou shalt be saved, and thy house" (Acts 16:31).

These are the verses that led me through the *door* of salvation and into the *assurance* of salvation: *"That if thou shalt confess with thy mouth the Lord Jesus, and shalt believe in thine heart that God hath raised Him from the dead, thou shalt be saved. For with the heart man believeth unto righteousness; and with the mouth confession is made unto salvation"* (Rom. 10:9, 10).

There is only one way to be saved, and that is the BIBLE way. Salvation is the gift of God, and the only way to come into possession of a gift is to receive it from the giver. *A gift cannot be bought.* If a price is paid or labor rendered in return, the gift is destroyed. It is not by works of righteousness which we can do, but by the finished work of Jesus that we are saved:

"Not by works of righteousness which we have done, but according to His mercy He saved us, by the washing of regeneration, and renewing of the Holy Ghost; Which He shed on us abundantly through Jesus Christ our Saviour" (Tit. 3:5, 6).

Regardless of who he may be, how wicked he has become — or how morally above reproach he may be — the only way anyone can be saved is clearly set forth in John 1:12, 13:

"... *As many as received Him, to them gave He power to become the sons of God, even to them that believe on His name: Which were born, not of blood, nor of the will of the flesh, nor of the will of man, but of God.*"

My dearly beloved, if you are not saved, humble your heart this moment and in your own words, in your own way, talk to the heavenly Father. Ask Him to save you in the name of Jesus, through the finished *work* of Jesus in His death, burial, resurrection, and ascension. Simply ask God to be merciful to you as a sinner and save you for Christ's sake. Pray it, believe it — and God will save you now.

IN CLOSING

Let us sum up what we have covered in our study of this portion of God's Word:

IN HIS LIFE, Jesus is our example: "For even hereunto were ye called: because Christ also suffered for us, leaving us an example, that ye should follow His steps" (I Pet. 2:21). Notice this Scripture does not say that Jesus was our *pattern*, but rather that He is our *EXAMPLE*. A pattern must be reproduced in exactness; but an example is "*that which may be reproduced in spirit.*"

It is true that believers will never be able to live as pure and sinless as Jesus lived; but we CAN follow in His steps and follow His example. (Do not misunderstand — Christ is not the example for sinners; He is the example for believers. It is utterly impossible for an unbeliever to follow the example of Christ.)

IN HIS DEATH, Jesus is our Redeemer: "The wages of sin is death" (Rom. 6:23). "... The soul that sinneth, it shall die" (Ezek. 18:4). "... When lust hath conceived, it bringeth

forth sin: and sin, when it is finished, bringeth forth death"
(James 1:15).

The Scriptures teach us that *"Christ died for our sins
according to the Scriptures"* (I Cor. 15:3). Any minister who
minimizes sin and treads lightly when he preaches on sin,
will also minimize the *atonement,* and will fail to preach the
blood atonement as the only escape from damnation. The
minister who preaches that sin is "just a mistake" will also
preach that one may be saved through strength of character
and practice of good works.

But the Word of God teaches that it is only through
shedding of blood that we find remission for sin, and "without
shedding of blood is no remission" (Heb. 9:22). The blood
of Jesus Christ cleanses us from all sin (I John 1:7). Jesus
paid the penalty, He died the death. He suffered in our
stead, He offered Himself for every sinner upon the face of
this earth — *and there is no other way for a sinner to be saved!*

In His life, Jesus is the example for believers — sons of
God; but only through His death can unbelievers be saved.
Jesus IS salvation and without Him there is no salvation. He
said, "No man cometh unto the Father but by me" (John
14:6).

IN HIS BURIAL, Jesus is our scapegoat. We noted
in Romans 4:25 that He was delivered for our offences. It was
our sins that nailed Jesus to the cross. In Leviticus we read
the account of the "scapegoat" of the Old Testament, and
while this is definitely Jewish, it may be used as an illustration for us. The priest stood with his hands upon the head
of the goat, confessing the sins of Israel, and the goat was
then led away into a land where no man lived.

Thus the scapegoat was a symbol in carrying the sins of
Israel into "a land that was uninhabited," putting them behind God's back, never to be remembered. So Jesus, the
Lamb of God without spot or blemish, died for our sins on
the cruel cross. In His shed blood, He paid the penalty

for our sin, and in His burial became our scapegoat, bearing
our sins away as far as the East is from the West. In His
burial He is the scapegoat of all who put their trust in His
death, burial, and resurrection.

IN HIS RESURRECTION, *Jesus is our justification*: He
was delivered because of our offences, but *He was raised for
our justification* (Rom. 4:25).

There is a song which we sing, and in which we find
these words: *"He tore the bars away,* Jesus, my Lord!" There
is not one particle of scriptural truth in that statement.
Jesus DID NOT tear away the bars of the tomb, nor did He
tear away the bars of death.

If a prisoner in the penitentiary tears the bars away and
escapes before he completes his sentence, he is still guilty —
even more so than before he escaped; but *JESUS was raised*
for our justification. Therefore, He did NOT tear the bars
away, He did not "break out" of the grave. He entered the
grave as prophesied. He spent three days and three nights
there — and when the allotted time was up, all things having
been fulfilled to bring about our justification, having met all
the demands of the law and satisfied the heart of God, *the
stone rolled away* and Jesus, answering for our justification,
walked out of the tomb. He did not *break* out — *He walked
out,* having paid sin's debt in full!

What IS Bible justification? Justification means that Christians stand before God just as though we had never sinned,
just as just as Jesus is just, because we stand before God IN
Christ Jesus. Justification means that the sins of the believer
are put behind God's back, cast into the depths of the sea,
carried "into a land uninhabited" — and there they are forgotten. God has forgotten that the born again believer has
ever sinned. Justification means that the believer stands before God with a record that is absolutely clean and without
spot. We are justified in His grace, through the finished work
of Jesus.

But there is more: This man Christ Jesus, Saviour of sinners, is now seated at the right hand of God the Father, and therefore, *in His ascension He is our head.* He is the head of the Church and every true believer is a member of His body. God recognizes the head and will therefore receive the members.

Believers need not fear nor dread the moment when they stand before God, because Jesus said, "If you confess me before men, I will confess you before my Father which is in heaven." He has ascended, He sits at the right hand of God the Father, and He is our Mediator, our head.

IN HIS SECOND COMING, Jesus is our hope. These are dark days — days when men's hearts are failing them for fear. We are living in days of sorrow, sadness, disappointment, and heartache. There are wars and rumors of wars; there are pestilences and earthquakes. These days are "the beginning of sorrows" (Matt. 24:8). Probably some are asking, "O Lord, how long? how long?"

We may rest assured that He IS coming. He promised, and He cannot lie. To His sad, discouraged disciples Jesus said, "Let not your heart be troubled: ye believe in God, believe also in me. In my Father's house are many mansions: if it were not so, I would have told you. *I go to prepare a place for YOU.* And if I go and prepare a place for you, *I will come again, and receive you unto myself;* that where I am, there ye may be also" (John 14:1-3).

God's Word promises, "This same Jesus, which is taken up from you into heaven, shall so come in like manner as ye have seen Him go into heaven" (Acts 1:11).

Paul said, "I would not have you to be ignorant, brethren, concerning them which are asleep, that ye sorrow not, even as others which have no hope. For if we believe that Jesus died and rose again, even so them also which sleep in Jesus will God bring with Him. For this we say unto you by the word of the Lord, that we which are alive and remain unto the coming of the Lord shall not prevent them which are asleep. For the Lord Himself shall descend from heaven with a shout, with the voice of the archangel, and with the trump of God: and the dead in Christ shall rise first: Then we which are alive and remain shall be caught up together with them in the clouds, to meet the Lord in the air: *and so shall we ever be with the Lord. Wherefore comfort one another with these words*" (I Thess. 4:13-18).

The last declaration in the Bible was made by none other than the Lord Jesus Christ: "He which testifieth these things saith, *Surely I come quickly.*"

The last prayer in the Bible is a prayer for the soon coming of Jesus. John the Beloved prayed, *"Even so, Come!"*

If we love the Lord as we should and if we are living as we should — as good stewards, good soldiers, living examples of Jesus — we, too, should be praying, "Even so, Come! *Come quickly, Lord Jesus!"*

In His living, Jesus is the *example* for the believer.

In His dying, He is the *Redeemer* of sinners.

In His burial, He is the believer's *scapegoat*.

In His bodily resurrection, He is our *justification*.

In His ascension, He is the *head of the Church*, and therefore the head of all believers.

In His second coming, He is the *hope* of the believer.

Do YOU know Jesus? If you do not, receive Him now!

Are you SAVED? If you are, bow your head and thank God for Jesus, your Saviour!

CHRIST OUR REDEEMER

CHRIST OUR REDEEMER

IN WHOM WE HAVE REDEMPTION THROUGH HIS BLOOD, THE forgiveness of sins, according to the riches of His grace" (Eph. 1:7).

"In whom we have redemption through His blood, even the forgiveness of sins" (Col. 1:14).

I am sure there are some who will ask, "Are not salvation and redemption one and the same? If Christ is our *Saviour*, is He not also our *Redeemer?*" As we study the Scriptures presented in this message, we will discover new aspects of His work, and of our condition as sons of God through His death.

The truth of the matter is, Christ accomplished redemption *before* He could be called *"Jesus"* (Saviour), before He could be *presented* as the Saviour of sinners. Jesus is able to *save* the sinner only because of His finished work on the cross, and God *receives* the sinner only on the basis of that finished work. Therefore, insofar as God is concerned, *redemption precedes* salvation.

You will notice that in the verses used as a text, the

word is not "Redeemer," but *redemption*. There are several verses in the New Testament, some of which will be pointed out in the message, which refer to Jesus as having redeemed us — and we do have redemption through His blood; but in the *Old Testament* Scriptures we find the term "Redeemer" used many times:

Job 19:25: "For I know that my *Redeemer* liveth, and that He shall stand at the latter day upon the earth."

Psalm 19:14: "Let the words of my mouth, and the meditation of my heart, be acceptable in thy sight, O Lord, my strength, and my *Redeemer*."

Psalm 78:35: "And they remembered that God was their rock, and the high God their *Redeemer*."

Isaiah 41:14: "Fear not, thou worm Jacob, and ye men of Israel: I will help thee, saith the Lord, and thy *Redeemer*, the Holy One of Israel."

Isaiah 43:14: "Thus saith the Lord, your Redeemer, the Holy One of Israel; For your sake I have sent to Babylon, and have brought down all their nobles, and the Chaldeans, whose cry is in the ships."

Isaiah 44:6: "Thus saith the Lord the King of Israel, and his Redeemer the Lord of hosts; I am the first, and I am the last; and beside me there is no God."

Isaiah 47:4: "As for our Redeemer, the Lord of hosts is His name, the Holy One of Israel."

Isaiah 49:26: "And I will feed them that oppress thee with their own flesh; and they shall be drunken with their own blood, as with sweet wine: and all flesh shall know that I the Lord am thy Saviour and thy Redeemer, the mighty One of Jacob."

There are many — yea, scores — of Scriptures in the Old Testament where the word "Redeemer" is used; and even though it is not used in the New Testament, Jesus is *presented* as our Redeemer in each of the New Testament books.

In Revelation we read that as the elders in heaven behold

the Lamb slain from the foundation of the world, the Lamb who is worthy to open the book, they sing a new song: "Thou art worthy to take the book and to open the seals thereof for thou wast slain and hast REDEEMED us to God by thy blood out of every kindred, and tongue, and people and nation" (Rev. 5:9).

It is sound Bible doctrine that in every dispensation God has been a Redeemer; He has brought redemption to men since Adam. Adam had nothing to do with the blood sacrifice that covered the shame of his nakedness. Innocent animals furnished the skins at the expense of their blood, and it was God who from those skins made coats for Adam and Eve.

In the Old Testament Scriptures, two words are used for "redemption." One of the words means "to buy back, to redeem through payment of ransom"; the other word used frequently in English is translated "to loose." In reality, they are used in the same sense throughout the Old Testament Scriptures, for if one is *bought back* because another pays the debt owed, then the one who is bought back at the expense of another is automatically *loosed* from the obligation that bound him.

In the New Testament there is only one Greek word translated "redeem" or "redemption," and the meaning of that word is "to release on payment of a ransom." The word has a twofold meaning: *Redemption* means "the payment of a ransom"; it means for someone to supply a sum of money to release one who has been kidnapped and held captive. The consequence is *deliverance* — the one being held captive is freed, and the person having been freed because of the ransom paid then passes into the state which is known as *having been redeemed*.

In the natural sense, the one who is redeemed enjoyed freedom and liberty until taken captive. The captors demanded a sum of money for ransom, and the person paying the ransom redeems the one held captive; who, after he is set free, is again in the position of having been redeemed, enjoying freedom and liberty.

THE STATE OF ALL MEN
BEFORE REDEMPTION

First, we must see why it was necessary that a Redeemer be provided. Why was it necessary for a ransom to be paid? Who was held captive, *and why?*

"Wherefore as by one man sin entered into the world, and death by sin; and so death passed upon all men, for that all have sinned" (Rom. 5:12).

"Therefore as by the offence of one, judgment came upon all men to condemnation . . ." (Rom. 5:18).

"For as by one man's disobedience many were made sinners . . ." (Rom. 5:19).

"That as sin hath reigned unto death . . ." (Rom. 5:21).

Satan is the author of sin, sin is the author of death, and death reigned over all men; but it goes deeper than that. God clearly laid down the rules for Adam to live by, but he knowingly stepped over God's rules and became a sinner. Thus through the deliberate disobedience of Adam, and through his fall, man became a sinner. Through man's sin and his fall, Satan acquired rights over mankind — *and SATAN held the power of death!*

"Forasmuch then as the children are partakers of flesh and blood, (Jesus) also Himself likewise took part of the same; that through death He might destroy him that had the power of death, THAT IS, THE DEVIL; and deliver them who through fear of death were all their lifetime subject to bondage" (Heb. 2:14, 15).

Whether we like to accept it or not, it is a Bible fact that *through Adam's sin* Satan became the one who had power to wield the hand of death — and death is the just judgment of a holy God. God clearly said to Adam, "The day you eat thereof you shall surely die." He did not eat the forbidden fruit in ignorance, he ate knowingly. Thus in Adam all die.

Because of Adam's sin the devil became "the prince of this world": "Now is the judgment of this world: now shall *the prince of this world* be cast out" (John 12:31). ". . . Of judgment, because *the prince of this world* is judged" (John 16:11).

Through the disobedience of Adam the devil became "the god of this world": "*in* whom *the god of this world* hath blinded the minds of them which believe not, lest the light of the glorious gospel of Christ, who is the image of God, should shine unto them" (II Cor. 4:4).

Satan is the "prince of the power of the air": "Wherein in time past ye walked according to the course of this world, according to *the prince of the power of the air,* the spirit that now worketh in the children of disobedience" (Eph. 2:2).

When the Lord called and commissioned Paul as minister to the Gentiles, He said to Paul, ". . . Rise, and stand upon thy feet: for I have appeared unto thee for this purpose, to make thee a minister and a witness both of these things which thou hast seen, and of those things in which I will appear unto thee; delivering thee from the people, and from the Gentiles, unto whom now I send thee, to open their eyes, and to turn them from darkness to light, and from the power of Satan unto God, that they may receive forgiveness of sins, and inheritance among them which are sanctified by faith that is in me" (Acts 26:16-18).

Notice carefully: ". . . *To turn them from darkness to light, from the power of Satan unto God, that they may receive forgiveness of sins.*" Whether we like to admit it or not, because of the disobedience of Adam, Satan holds all men captive under his Satanic power until they are delivered — yea, *redeemed* — by the Redeemer, the Lord Jesus Christ: "Who hath delivered us from the power of darkness, and hath

translated us into the kingdom of His dear Son, in whom
we have redemption through His blood, even the forgiveness
of sins" (Col. 1:13, 14).

Unbelievers are helpless and hopeless until, by faith,
they trust in the finished work of Jesus Christ. We are fallen
creatures. Because of sin we are under the *penalty* of sin,
and that penalty is DEATH! Since we are sinners, we are
under the power of Satan — the prince of this world, the god
of this age, the prince of the power of the air. The unbeliever
is not controlled and possessed by a captor of flesh and blood,
but by mighty powers of spiritual wickedness — yea, even
Satan himself.

The sinner could never have provided his own ransom
because he is held captive by Satan, bound and helpless; and
had Someone else not paid the ransom there would have
been no hope, *ever*, for the unbeliever. Someone else of necessity had to provide the ransom, for it was expedient that one
die for the people.

Man in his natural state fails to meet God's requirements,
fails to answer God's holy claims. Therefore, since the natural
man cannot receive the things of God (because they are
spiritually discerned), and since from within we cannot provide the ransom to pay the redemption price, we are under
the penalty of sin until delivered by another — our RE-
DEEMER, Christ Jesus, Saviour of sinners.

Not only is the unbeliever under *the penalty of sin* — he is
also under the dominion of Satan, a subject of Satan's kingdom. Jesus describes unbelievers as children of the devil: "Ye
are of your father the devil, and the lusts of your father ye
will do. He was a murderer from the beginning, and abode
not in the truth, because there is no truth in him. When
he speaketh a lie, he speaketh of his own: for he is a liar, and
the father of it" (John 8:44).

If you will make a careful study of the twenty-eighth
chapter of Ezekiel and the fourteenth chapter of Isaiah, you

will learn that the devil, as we know him today, originated because of jealousy. The being whom we know as Satan was, in his original state, *"Lucifer, the shining one, son of the morning."* He was "the anointed cherub that covereth." But he became jealous of God and decided that he would brainwash the angels and lead them in revolt *against God,* overthrow the Almighty and take His throne!

But the plan failed. Almighty God cast Satan out. Jesus said, *"I beheld Satan as lightning fall from heaven"* (Luke 10:18); and Jude 6 tells us that the angels he led astray are now "reserved in everlasting chains under darkness unto the judgment of the great day."

Satan was not willing to be subordinate to God even though he was the anointed cherub who "walked up and down in the midst of the stones of fire," in the very presence of God and around the heavenly throne. He was jealous, envious, he coveted God's throne — and God threw him out of heaven.

Satan entered the Garden of Eden with a heart filled with jealousy, for God had created man in His own image — a living soul; and God fellowshipped with him. Satan could not produce a living soul such as God had created in Adam, and he was jealous; so he set about to corrupt man. He entered the garden, suggested to Eve that God had not told her the whole story and that the reason the Creator did not want her and Adam to eat the forbidden fruit was because He knew their eyes would be opened and they would be "as gods." That is what *Satan* wanted to be — he wanted to be God.

So he talked to Eve — and sad to say, *she listened.* Then Adam listened, they ate of the fruit of which God had forbidden them to eat. They sinned — and because of Adam's disobedience sin's penalty of death moved in upon him. Thus, through Adam's sin all men are sinners. There is none righteous — no, not one, for all have sinned and come short of the glory of God.

Man in his natural state, then, has no claim upon God. Because of his sin, his just reward is death; but because God is rich in mercy, and because of His great love to mankind, the Redeemer was brought down to man. But suppose we let the Scriptures say it for us:

Ephesians 2:1-10: "And you hath He quickened, who were dead in trespasses and sins: Wherein in time past ye walked according to the course of this world, according to the prince of the power of the air, the spirit that now worketh in the children of disobedience: among whom also we all had our conversation in times past in the lusts of our flesh, fulfilling the desires of the flesh and of the mind; and were by nature the children of wrath, even as others. But God, who is rich in mercy for His great love wherewith He loved us, even when we were dead in sins, hath quickened us together with Christ, (by grace ye are saved;) And hath raised us up together, and made us sit together in heavenly places in Christ Jesus: That in the ages to come He might shew the exceeding riches of His grace in His kindness toward us through Christ Jesus. For by grace are ye saved through faith; and that not of yourselves: it is the gift of God: Not of works, lest any man should boast. For we are His workmanship, created in Christ Jesus unto good works, which God hath before ordained that we should walk in them."

Look at the horrible condition of the sinner: Dead in trespasses and sin, walking according to the course of the world, living according to the dictates of the devil, having conversation in the lust of the flesh, fulfilling the desires of the flesh and by nature the child of Satan!

BUT GOD!!! Never forget that in the beginning, before ever God laid the foundation of this earth or created the dust from which Adam was made, before God planted the Garden of Eden or created man to occupy it, *He had already planned and perfected redemption!* God's great love, rich in mercy, reached out even when we were dead in sin, strengthless and hopeless, and provided the Redeemer:

"Forasmuch as ye know that ye were not redeemed with corruptible things, as silver and gold, from your vain conversation received by tradition from your fathers; But with the precious blood of Christ, as of a lamb without blemish and without spot: Who verily was foreordained before the foundation of the world, but was manifest in these last times for you, who by Him do believe in God, that raised Him up from the dead, and gave Him glory; that your faith and hope might be in God. Seeing ye have purified your souls in obeying the truth through the Spirit unto unfeigned love of the brethren, see that ye love one another with a pure heart, fervently: being born again, not of corruptible seed, but of incorruptible, by the Word of God, which liveth and abideth for ever" (1 Pet. 1:18-23).

THE "HOW" OF REDEMPTION

I want us to see the method through which God brought about our redemption and I want us to see the *price* of redemption — just what ransom was demanded to set the captives free?

While here upon earth Jesus said to His disciples, " . . . The Son of man came not to be ministered unto, but to minister, and to give His life a ransom for many" (Matt. 20:28). Paul declares the same truth in other words, in I Timothy 2:6: "Who gave Himself a ransom for all, to be testified in due time."

Jesus gave Himself. No man took His life — He laid it down. He GAVE His life on the cross to pay the ransom demanded to set the captive free from the penalty of sin and the power of Satan.

Remember our text: *"In whom we have redemption through His blood, even the forgiveness of sins, according to the riches of His grace.*" The significance of the statements in Matthew 20:28 and I Timothy 2:6 is explained in Leviticus 17:11: ". . . The life of the flesh IS IN THE BLOOD: and I have given it to you upon the altar to make an atonement for your souls: for it is the BLOOD that maketh an atonement for the soul."

Therefore, in the New Testament we read, "Without shedding of blood is no remission" (Heb. 9:22), and "The blood of Jesus Christ (God's) Son cleanseth us from all sin" (I John 1:7). The life of the flesh is in the blood, and it was the blood of Christ that provided the value that made possible our ransom paid. The blood of Jesus was the price paid for redemption. Jesus our Redeemer paid the redemption price — (He was the only One in heaven or earth who *could* pay it) — and thus Paul declares, *"IN WHOM* (Jesus) we have redemption through His blood, the forgiveness of sins. . ."* (Eph. 1:7).

I Peter 1:19 refers to the blood of Jesus as *"precious"* — a word used by a tenderhearted, loving mother in speaking to her newborn babe, or by lovers, ready to be married, their hearts knit together as one. Peter could have said, "The *powerful* blood" — and truly, there IS power in the blood of Jesus. He could have said "The *cleansing* blood" — and truly the blood of Jesus *cleanses* us. He could have used many adjectives to describe the blood of Jesus, but to Peter there was no word in all the languages of all the world that could take the place of "PRECIOUS."

Consider the man who used this word. Had it been used by a tender, compassionate mother it would not seem so strange; but Peter was a fisherman, and during the first days of his experience with Jesus he was "in the rough." He went so far on one occasion as to curse and declare that he did not *know* the Lord — and moments later, in repentance, he was weeping bitter tears! Bible history tells us that at the close of Peter's ministry, he was crucified head downward for his testimony for Christ. Whether this be true or not is immaterial. What IS of interest is that Peter knew no word in any language that would describe the blood of Jesus and its meaning for him as fully as the word "precious" — *the PRECIOUS blood of Christ.*

And truly the blood of Jesus IS precious, for it meets all the claims of Jehovah God — the God of all creation, He who was in the beginning, He who has no ending, the God who cannot be tempted with evil. The blood of Jesus satisfied the holiness and righteousness of God and laid the foundation for the salvation of sinners. Through the blood of Jesus Christ, God can still be just and holy, perfect and sinless — and yet justify a sinner who deserves to burn in hell!

The blood of Jesus Christ not only *satisfied God's claims,* but the shedding of His blood glorified God. Jesus said, "I lay down my life for the sheep . . . therefore doth my Father love me" (John 10:15 and 17).

In the shedding of His blood, Jesus glorified God in that *through the blood* hell-bound sinners can become sons of God; and through the shedding of His blood Jesus brings glory to Himself because through His blood sinners become believers and are brought to Him — yea, they are united to His body through the baptism of the Holy Spirit. Christ is the head of the body, and every believer is a member of that body (Eph. 5:30; I Cor. 12:12). When we believe on Jesus we become God's children, and as His children we are heirs of God and joint-heirs with Christ: "And if children, then heirs; heirs of God, and joint-heirs with Christ; if so be that we suffer with Him, that we may be also glorified to-gether" (Rom. 8:17).

Here is the picture: In the Garden of Eden, because of Adam's sin, Satan captured man and became the god of this world, the prince of the power of the air. He became the one who strikes the death-blow — an authority that moved to him because of man's sin. But Jesus Christ the Son of

God took a body of flesh, and in that flesh He conquered him who had the power of death and took from him the keys of death, hell, and the grave: *"I am He that liveth, and was dead; and, behold, I am alive for evermore, Amen; and have the keys of hell and of death"* (Rev. 1:18).

The ransom demanded for the release of the captives of Satan was nothing less than the blood of the Lamb, the Christ of God; but God so loved sinners that He *set forth* His Son to be a propitiation through faith in His blood, to declare God's righteousness and to make it possible for God to remain righteous and yet justify the ungodly when they put their faith in the shed blood and the finished work of the Lamb of God.

All who are covered by the blood are sheltered and safe from the judgment of a holy God upon sin. The blood of Jesus Christ cleanses and washes away all sin as though it had never been.

A BEAUTIFUL PICTURE OF REDEMPTION IN THE OLD TESTAMENT

When God was ready to send the death angel through the land of Egypt because Pharaoh had not hearkened to His Word, it was a divine necessity, because of God's covenant with His people, that He deal with them in righteousness; but He must also judge *Egypt* in righteous judgment. God *cannot* judge otherwise.

Egypt deserved the judgment that was about to be poured out upon her; but how could God strike the Egyptians *and yet deal with Israel in righteousness,* not meting out to Israel the same destructive blow of judgment? God spoke to Pharaoh in these words: ". . . I will put a *division* between my people and thy people: to morrow shall this sign be" (Ex. 8:23).

The same Hebrew word used here for *division* is trans-

lated "redemption" in Psalm 111:9 and Psalm 130:7; so —
we could read here, "And I will put a *redemption* between
my people and thy people." That is exactly what God did.

After speaking thus to Pharaoh, God spoke to His servant
Moses. Moses called for all the elders of Israel and said to
them, "Draw out and take you a lamb according to your
families, and kill the passover. And ye shall take a bunch
of hyssop, and dip it in the blood that is in the bason, and
strike the lintel and the two side posts with the blood that is
in the bason; and none of you shall go out at the door of his
house until the morning. For the Lord will pass through to
smite the Egyptians; and when He seeth the blood upon the
lintel, and on the two side posts, the Lord will pass over the
door, and will not suffer the destroyer to come in unto your
house to smite you" (Ex. 12:21-23).

Jehovah redeemed the people of Israel by the blood.
The blood on the doorposts and over the door point to the
blood of the Lamb of God, shed on the old rugged cross:
". . . John seeth Jesus coming unto him, and saith, Behold
the Lamb of God, which taketh away the sin of the world"
(John 1:29).

Study the portion of God's Word just quoted from
Exodus. Tremendous truth is set forth here. The command
was, "**Take** a lamb, kill the lamb, catch the blood in a basin.
Then take hyssop, dip it in the blood, put the blood on the
lintel and the two sideposts of the door — and the Lord will
pass over the door. BUT NONE OF YOU SHALL GO OUT
AT THE DOOR OF HIS HOUSE UNTIL THE MORNING!"
It was a divine imperative that the Israelites *remain in the
house* marked by the blood.

The believer becomes a member of the body of Christ
through the blood of Jesus — the pierced side, the nails in His
hands and feet, the thorns on His brow. Through the shed
blood of Jesus we are protected — but those who are *outside*
of the covering blood are NOT protected. God's invitation

was to all Israel, and if any chose to refuse the invitation they must suffer the consequences. They were to sprinkle the blood as instructed, and then remain behind the blood-marked door. *Christ* is the door to salvation. He said, "By me, if any man enter in, he shall be saved."

The Lamb of God shed His blood for the sins of the world (I John 2:1, 2). In John 3:16 we learn that God so loved the world that He gave His only begotten Son, that *whosoever believeth* . . . should have everlasting life. This is the one imperative. We must *believe,* we must have faith, we must trust in His shed blood.

"Whom God hath set forth to be a propitiation THROUGH FAITH in His blood . . ." (Rom. 3:25).

But redemption goes further than just the payment of ransom. The ransom must be paid — and, as we have already seen, it WAS paid by the blood of Jesus on the cross. The Israelites were safely sheltered in their homes where the door was marked by the blood; but *Israel was not redeemed,* not even while they were in the house with the door closed and the blood on the lintel and the two sideposts. They were perfectly SAFE under the shelter of the blood *as long as they were in their homes in Egypt;* but when they left those homes, Pharaoh decided that he would destroy them — and *the completion of the redemption of Israel* was affected when God stretched out His mighty arm and brought them OUT of the land of Egypt with all of their people, their children, and their cattle. Not one hoof was left behind (Ex. 10:26). God led them out of Egypt through the Red Sea, and in the process He completely destroyed Pharaoh and his great hosts of mighty warriors.

How was this done? Through a miracle that only God Almighty could have made possible. Surely you know the story: The children of Israel were facing the Red Sea, the mountains on one side of them and Pharaoh behind them. It seemed as though total destruction would be their fate.

But Moses looked to God. God answered, rolled back the waters of the Red Sea, and the children of Israel crossed on dry ground. But when Pharaoh and his armies, in pursuit of God's people, entered the basin of the sea where the waters had been rolled back, God let go the waters — and Pharaoh and his mighty hosts were drowned: "And the waters returned, and covered the chariots, and the horsemen, and all the host of Pharaoh that came into the sea after them; *there remained not so much as one of them!*" (Ex. 14:28).

Jehovah God, in all of His holiness and righteousness, having been satisfied on the basis of the shed blood placed on the lintel and the doorposts as He had instructed Moses, could now act as the Deliverer of His people *because of the blood* that brought satisfaction to Him as the holy Judge. Because the Israelites obeyed concerning the blood, God brought them out of Egypt by His mighty delivering power.

The children of Israel could not sing in the land of Egypt; but when they were out of that land of bondage they sang:

"Then sang Moses and the children of Israel this song unto the Lord, and spake, saying, I will sing unto the Lord, for He hath triumphed gloriously: the horse and his rider hath He thrown into the sea. The Lord is my strength and song, and He is become my salvation: He is my God, and I will prepare Him an habitation; my father's God, and I will exalt Him.

"The Lord is a man of war: the Lord is His name. Pharaoh's chariots and his host hath he cast into the sea: his chosen captains also are drowned in the Red Sea. The depths have covered them: they sank into the bottom as a stone. Thy right hand, O Lord, is become glorious in power: thy right hand, O Lord, hath dashed in pieces the enemy. And in the greatness of thine excellency thou hast overthrown them that rose up against thee: thou sentest forth thy wrath, which consumed them as stubble. And with the blast of thy nostrils the waters were gathered together, the floods stood upright as an heap, and the depths were congealed in the heart of the sea.

"The enemy said, I will pursue, I will overtake, I will divide the spoil; my lust shall be satisfied upon them; I will draw my sword, My hand shall destroy them. Thou didst blow with thy wind, the sea covered them: they sank as lead in the mighty waters.

"Who is like unto thee, O Lord, among the gods? Who is like thee, glorious in holiness, fearful in praises, doing wonders? Thou stretchedst out thy right hand, the earth swallowed them. Thou in thy mercy hast led forth the people which thou hast redeemed: thou hast guided them in thy strength unto thy holy habitation" (Ex. 15:1-13).

On the other side of the Red Sea, Israel was a redeemed people, and GOD was their Redeemer. The same is true in the life of a believer. Through the blood of Jesus Christ the believer has not only been redeemed from the bondage and captive power of sin, but the blood of the Lamb also delivers from the daily danger of falling victim to sin, as shown in the picture of Israel with high mountains on one side, the Red Sea before them and Pharaoh behind them. From the human standpoint they were without hope insofar as victory was concerned.

The same is true in the life of the believer. If God saved us and then left it up to us to live a Christian life in natural strength, Christianity would be a complete failure. But Christianity is Christ FOR the *sinner,* Christ IN the *believer,* and Christ the Mediator *on behalf* of the believer. In the blood we are saved, kept, delivered — and because of the blood we will be presented faultless to God the Father — but only on the merit of the shed blood of Jesus.

For Israel, the placing of the blood on the lintels and sideposts of the door, and the crossing of the Red Sea were two separate events; their deliverance happened in two stages. But in the case of the born again believer, in the death, burial, and resurrection of Christ we have the fulness of God *and we are complete in Him.* He is our sufficiency. He saves us from the *penalty* of sin, He saves us from the *power* of sin, and in the by-and-by He will save us from the very *presence* of sin.

THE "HOW" OF OUR DELIVERANCE

In the only begotten Son, God dealt with the question of our guilt and also our evil nature: " . . . God, sending His own Son in the likeness of sinful flesh, and for sin, condemned sin in the flesh" (Rom. 8:3). In the death of Jesus, God judged sin from the standpoint of the root, and also from the standpoint of the fruit.

Through His death, Christ personally met and broke the power of Satan, with the result that when the sinner believes from the heart, accepting the finished work of Christ, he is brought out of the old condition — the nature received from Adam in which all men are born sinners; and, through the resurrection of Jesus, is brought into a new life where there is no condemnation. The believer also possesses a life that through the law of the Spirit of life in Christ Jesus makes him free from the law of sin and death.

"There is therefore now no condemnation to them which are in Christ Jesus, who walk not after the flesh, but after the Spirit. For the law of the Spirit of life in Christ Jesus hath made me free from the law of sin and death. For what the law could not do, in that it was weak through the flesh, God sending His own Son in the likeness of sinful flesh, and for sin, condemned sin in the flesh" (Rom. 8:1-3).

Notice the clear language, the positive statements: *There is NO condemnation to them which are in Christ Jesus . . . What the law could not do because of the weakness of the flesh, God did in flesh in the Person of Jesus Christ . . . Through His shed blood we are delivered from the ROOT of sin as well as from the branch that bears the FRUITS of sin.*

His blood not only cleanses us from SIN (singular) but He is also the propitiation for our SINS (plural). Read John 1:29 and I John 2:1, 2.

". . . Ye are not in the flesh, but in the Spirit, if so be that the Spirit of God dwell in you. Now if any man have not the Spirit of Christ, he is none of His" (Rom. 8:9).

"Therefore if any man be in Christ, he is a new creature: old things are passed away; behold, all things are become new" (II Cor. 5:17).

The redemption we possess through faith in the finished work of Jesus is complete. God provided redemption is His Son and in the Son all the claims of God the Father have been met and completely satisfied through the shed blood of the Lamb without spot or blemish. Therefore, when we exercise faith in His shed blood, we are delivered — or brought out of — the kingdom of darkness and placed into the kingdom of light (Col. 1:13). We are taken out of our old condition and placed in the body of Christ (II Cor. 5:17; Col. 3:3).

We are not *in the process* of passing from death unto life, we are *already PASSED* from death unto life. The death and judgment that sin brings are behind us. In God's sight, born again believers are no longer in the flesh; we are new creations — not sons of the first Adam, but sons of the second Adam, the Lord Jesus Christ, who paid sin's debt and purchased redemption through His blood.

Paul testified, "I am crucified with Christ: nevertheless I live; yet not I, but Christ liveth in me: and the life which I now live in the flesh I live by the faith of the Son of God, who loved me, and gave Himself for me" (Gal. 2:20). Since believers have died with Christ, every tie that bound us to the Adamic condition has been snapped, broken, and forever rendered void through His blood. We are now in Christ, Christ is in us, and we sit with Him in heavenly places. We are hid with Christ in God, sealed by the Holy Ghost until the day of redemption (Eph. 4:30).

Believers live in assurance. We do not think or "just suppose" — we KNOW — that we have passed from death unto life. We know this for many reasons. John said, "We know that we have passed from death unto life, because we love the brethren . . . " (I John 3:14). Jesus said to His disciples, "By this shall all men know that ye are my disciples, if ye have love one to another" (John 13:35).

Since we know that we are sons of God, we also know that ALL things work together for good to those who love God and are called according to His purpose — and we know that the purpose of God is to conform us to the image of His dear Son. Every believer is destined to be conformed to the image of Christ. Why? *"That HE might be the firstborn among many brethren."* Therefore, with hearts filled with assurance and joy, we ask, *"If God be FOR us, who CAN be against us?"* (Rom. 8:31).

We have the blessed assurance that *"neither death, nor life, nor angels, nor principalities, nor powers, nor things present, nor things to come, nor height, nor depth, NOR ANY OTHER CREATURE, shall be able to separate us from the love of God, which is in Christ Jesus our Lord"* (Rom. 8:38, 39).

THERE IS MORE

It is a sure Bible fact that we are redeemed, spirit and soul. We are redeemed from the *penalty* of sin — death. We are redeemed and kept from the *power* of sin (I Cor. 10:13; I John 5:4). But there is a third stage of redemption yet future — *the redemption of our bodies.*

Shall we look again at the experience in Egypt? God's chosen people were brought out of Egypt through the Red Sea, fully delivered from the annihilation Pharaoh would have inflicted upon them. Had not God worked a miracle and rolled back the waters of the Red Sea, Israel would have perished. They crossed over the Red Sea on dry ground because of the miracle of God, *but they wandered in the wilderness for forty long, wearisome years!*

We are *redeemed,* we *do* possess divine nature, and the Holy Spirit abides in our hearts; but we wait" for the adoption, to wit, the redemption of our body" (Rom. 8:23). Even spiritually minded, fully dedicated believers are still walking in the wilderness of this world. We are not OF the world, but we are certainly IN it. And because of our bodies of flesh we are definitely linked with a groaning, travailing creation. Even those of us who have the firstfruits of the Spirit groan within ourselves, waiting for that glorious day when our bodies will be redeemed (Rom. 8:18-25).

Paul said, "For our conversation is in heaven; from whence also we look for the Saviour, the Lord Jesus Christ: Who shall change our vile body, that it may be fashioned like unto His glorious body, according to the working whereby He is able even to subdue all things unto Himself" (Phil. 3:20, 21).

Only then will we fully realize how marvelous and glorious is our redemption! Through His shed blood Jesus paid the ransom, provided deliverance for soul, spirit, and body, and the redemption purchased at the tremendous price of His blood is complete and perfect.

We should never forget for one moment that this glorious redemption was purchased for us with His precious blood. We say those words — but do we really know what we are saying? Do we really appreciate the meaning of those words? Do we really see the Lamb of God — arrested, beaten, spit upon, His beard plucked out by the roots, crowned with thorns and nailed to a rugged cross? Do we see Him as He literally laid His life down, and went down under all the wrath of a holy God — wrath that should have fallen upon us because of our sins? Christ knew no sin, yet HE WAS MADE TO BE SIN for us, that we might become the righteousness of God in Him.

Do we really understand the fact that Jesus was MADE sin for us. He not only BORE our sin, but God the Father made Him to BE sin for us, that God could be righteous and yet justify the ungodly through their faith in the shed blood of the Lamb. All praise, adoration, and worship should be directed "unto Him that loved us, and washed us from our sins in His own blood, and hath made us kings and priests unto God and His Father; to Him be glory and dominion for ever and ever. Amen" (Rev. 1:5, 6).

"But we see Jesus, who was made a little lower than the angels for the suffering of death, crowned with glory and honour; that He by the grace of God should taste death for every man" (Heb. 2:9). Greek authorities tell us that the words here translated "every man" in their full meaning reach *beyond MAN* and could have been translated "every *thing.*" There are other Scriptures which support this statement.

"That in the dispensation of the fulness of times He might gather together in one all things in Christ, both which are in heaven, and which are on earth; even in Him" (Eph. 1:10).

"Thou hast put all things in subjection under His feet. For in that He put all in subjection under Him, He left nothing that is not put under Him. But now we see not yet all things put under Him" (Heb. 2:8).

"Again, the kingdom of heaven is like unto treasures hid in a field; the which when a man hath found, he hideth, and for joy thereof goeth and selleth all that he hath, *and buyeth that field*" (Matt. 13:44).

In II Peter 2:1 we read, "But there were false prophets also among the people, even as there shall be false teachers among you, who privily shall bring in damnable heresies, even *denying the Lord that bought them* and bring upon themselves swift destruction." We have these false prophets with us today, but we must remember that "all things were created by Him and for Him," whether in heaven or on earth,

and one glorious day there will be a NEW creation that will
be completely delivered from the curse.

A TRUTH WHICH BELIEVERS NEED TO SEE AND ACCEPT

Since Jesus has done so much for us, and since redemption's cost was so high, what is the believer's responsibility
toward Him?

In the first place, we need to acknowledge that we are
not our own. We are bought with a price and we belong to
Him who redeemed us at the expense of His blood: "But now
thus saith the Lord that created thee, O Jacob, and He that
formed thee, O Israel, Fear not: for I have redeemed thee, I
have called thee by thy name; thou art mine" (Isa. 43:1).

It is a grand and glorious privilege to believe on Jesus
Christ, to accept His finished work, and thereby become a son
of God; but as grand and glorious as that privilege is, there
is an equally great and grave responsibility that rests upon us!
Jesus acquired us as His possession through His shed blood,
and He holds an indisputable title. That is why, from the
inspired pen of the Apostle Paul, we read, "Who shall lay
anything to the charge of God's elect? It is God that justifieth.
Who is he that condemneth? It is Christ that died, yea rather,
that is risen again, who is even at the right hand of God,
who also maketh intercession for us" (Rom. 8:33, 34).

Our privilege is marvelous, but our responsibility is heavy,
for we are a distinct and separate people on earth: ". . . Ye are
a chosen generation, a royal priesthood, an holy nation, a
peculiar people; that ye should shew forth the praises of
Him who hath called you out of darkness into His marvellous
light" (I Pet. 2:9).

Since we are a special and a peculiar people, purchased
by the blood of the Lamb, Paul warns us, "What? Know ye
not that your body is the temple of the Holy Ghost which is

in you, which ye have of God, and ye are not your own? For ye are bought with a price: Therefore glorify God in your body, and in your spirit, which are God's" (I Cor. 6:19, 20).

So we see that the Lord not only owns our soul and spirit, but He also owns our body. He bought ALL of us. Therefore, in our body we are to display a Christian attitude, we are to live as nearly like Jesus lived as is possible, through His abundant grace and wisdom. We are to be blameless in whatsoever we are doing, and do all to the glory of God.

In Romans 12:1, 2 we read, "I beseech you therefore, brethren, by the mercies of God, that ye present your bodies a living sacrifice, holy, acceptable unto God, *which is your reasonable service.* And be not conformed to this world: but be ye transformed by the renewing of your mind, that ye may prove what is that good, and acceptable, and perfect, will of God."

When we have presented our bodies to God, yielding each of our members as instruments of righteousness, we have done nothing about which to boast; for since this is our "reasonable service" it would be *unreasonable* not to do so. When we have yielded completely to God — soul, spirit, and body — we have given Him only our reasonable service.

What a glorious fact, what a tremendous, divine miracle; that God can take these bodies of ours which once were tools of Satan — inhabited by him, fulfilling the lust of the flesh and by nature the children of wrath — and through the redemption that is in Christ He can put Himself on display in this world, that God might be glorified in us! In Matthew 5:16 Jesus instructs us, "Let your light so shine before men, that they may see your good works, and glorify your Father which is in heaven."

Jesus explained to His disciples, "Except a corn of wheat fall into the ground and die, it abideth alone: but if it die, it bringeth forth much fruit" (John 12:24). Satan did not realize what he was doing when he caused "the corn of wheat"

(Christ) to fall into the ground! For through His death, millions have been born into the family of God, and today there is not just ONE who is declaring God and making manifest the peace that God gives, but because of the shed blood of Jesus there are millions who have given soul, spirit, and body to Him. There are many on earth today who, in the words of Paul, are "living epistles read of men" (II Cor. 3:2).

In II Corinthians 4:8-10 Paul said, "We are troubled on every side, yet not distressed; we are perplexed, but not in despair; persecuted, but not forsaken; cast down, but not destroyed; always bearing about in the body the dying of the Lord Jesus, *that the life also of Jesus might be made manifest in our body.*"

Romans 6:13 commands us, "Neither yield ye your members as instruments of unrighteousness unto sin: but yield yourselves unto God, as those that are alive from the dead, and your members as instruments of righteousness unto God."

THE REDEEMED ALSO HAVE A NEGATIVE RESPONSIBILITY

I Corinthians 7:23 declares, "Ye are bought with a price; be not ye the servants of men!" Since we are redeemed it is our responsibility to deny, disown, and reject every authority or power that would conflict with the authority of Christ over us. However, Paul is not teaching here that we are to be slackers as having to do with those in authority over us from the standpoint of our jobs, but simply that we are to refrain from the fear of man, insofar as granting the wishes of man over and above the authority of God is concerned. Regarding the spiritual aspect of such service, we read, "For he that is called in the Lord, being a servant, is the Lord's freeman: likewise also he that is called, being free, is Christ's servant" (I Cor. 7:22).

In Colossians 3:23 and 24 Paul adds words enforcing the same truth: "And whatsoever ye do, do it heartily, as to the Lord, and not unto men; knowing that of the Lord ye shall receive the reward of the inheritance: for ye serve the Lord Christ." Whatever our position as we travel through this wilderness on earth, we must never forget that we belong to Christ, He purchased us with His blood, and we must keep our eyes on Him. He is our Lord as well as our Redeemer, and our first allegiance must be always to Him.

FURTHER RESPONSIBILITY OF THE REDEEMED

Jesus willingly gave Himself to redeem us, that He might purify unto Himself a peculiar people, anxious to do good works to His name's honor and glory. His object was to redeem us from all evil, sin, and iniquity — from its power and also from its habits or practices. "For sin shall not have dominion over you: ye are not under the law, but under grace" (Rom. 6:14).

We should not only refrain from the practice of sin, knowing that we are delivered from its power; but we should also go a step further and be anxious and zealous to do good works. Redemption separates us from evil, takes us out of the kingdom of darkness and places us in the kingdom of light, removes us from the family of Satan and places us in the family of God — but it goes further: We are not only separated FROM the evil one — we are separated UNTO CHRIST.

We are a "peculiar people," but the word *peculiar* does not mean that we are to be *queer*. We are to be peculiar from the standpoint of our habits of life, the company we keep and the language we use — our conduct in general. Christians should stand out in this dark world as a beacon shines on a dark night. We are a peculiar people who should be known because of our zeal for good works, works that will glorify *God*.

Let us hear Peter's testimony concerning this fact of redemption: "And if ye call on the Father, who without respect of persons judgeth according to every man's work, pass the time of your sojourning here in fear: Forasmuch as ye know that ye were not redeemed with corruptible things, as silver and gold, from your vain conversation received by tradition from your fathers; with the precious blood of Christ, as of a lamb without blemish and without spot" (I Pet. 1:17-19).

Peter places us in the presence of God the Father. He places us there as pilgrims on a sojourn through this wilderness of sin; but he declares that we should pass the time of our pilgrimage in fear. Christians cannot possess that fear apart from recognition of God's holiness, and knowledge that our works will be judged *according* to His holiness. True believers, redeemed by the blood, have been brought out of the "Egypt" of sin, and as we pass through this wilderness we are to maintain holiness, because *God* is holy: "Because it is written, Be ye holy; for I am holy" (I Pet. 1:16).

We are redeemed to God, therefore God requires us to walk in a way that is suitable and acceptable to Him. There is no room for selfishness or self-interest in the life of a spiritually minded believer. We are to live and conduct ourselves as becometh the holiness and character of God. We are to get in the yoke with Jesus and come alongside. In the words of Paul, "Follow His steps."

This divine fact should create within us a spirit of watchfulness. We should abstain from the very appearance of evil; we should walk worthy of the vocation wherein we are called, living in godly fear — not fearing God as we would fear an enemy, but with godly fear that will cause us to always recognize His all-seeing eye as observing our every action.

As we travel this pilgrim way, we are to be looking onward and upward to the day when our redemption will be complete — that glorious morning when we will receive "the redemption of the purchased possession, unto the praise of His glory" (Eph. 1:14).

The believer who studies to show himself approved unto God, and who, through consecration, study, and prayer has become a *spiritually-minded* believer, is not a babe in Christ but is growing by grace into the fulness of the spiritual man. Such a one is looking to that day when he will fully participate in the heritage that belongs to Christ our Redeemer — an inheritance to which Christ has a right, because through His own blood He purchased all things to Himself.

That glorious day will not come until He, by His power, has put all enemies under His feet — and then, when He shall have gathered together ALL the co-heirs, those who have received Him as Redeemer, with them He will enjoy the fullness of that which He purchased with His blood.

God saves us for Christ's sake (Eph. 4:32), and we are not only looking forward to the coming of Christ and the first resurrection when we will be like Him, but we are also looking forward to that glorious day when we, being glorified together with Christ our Redeemer, will experience our estate as joint-heirs with Him and will enter with our Redeemer into the possession of the wealth, glory, and blessedness that Jesus purchased through His death.

Believers are "accepted in the Beloved" to the praise of the glory of His (God's) grace; but our share with Christ as joint-heirs in His inheritance will be to the praise of His (Christ's) glory. If this divine fact breaks in upon your soul, it will be extremely difficult for you to hold back tears of joy and shouts of praises to God for all that He has purchased for us through the blood of Jesus Christ.

Not only are WE looking forward to that glorious morning when we will become joint-heirs with Christ in all of His heavenly fulness, but HE, too, is looking forward to that day, waiting for that moment when He can give us the full accomplishment of His shed blood. To give us the fulness of that which He accomplished is the uppermost desire of His heart as He sits at the right hand of God the Father, interceding for His children. He testified this fact in His own words in His intercessory prayer: "Father, I will that they also, WHOM THOU HAST GIVEN ME, be with me where I am; that they may behold my glory, which thou hast given me: for thou lovedst me before the foundations of the world" (John 17:24).

Words cannot describe the joy that it brings to my heart to know that Jesus is anxiously looking forward to that day when He can give to His own the fulness of His glory and His riches, and *God the Father* is joyously awaiting that glorious day when HE can display to all creation the riches of His grace in Christ Jesus:

"But God, who is rich in mercy, for His great love wherewith He loved us, even when we were dead in sins, hath quickened us together with Christ, (by grace ye are saved;) And hath raised us up together, and made us sit together in heavenly places in Christ Jesus: THAT IN THE AGES (eternity of eternities) TO COME HE MIGHT SHEW THE EXCEEDING RICHES OF HIS GRACE IN HIS KINDNESS TOWARD US THROUGH CHRIST JESUS" (Eph. 2:4-7).

What a glorious day that will be — for God the Father, for God the Son, for the saints, and for all creation!

IN CLOSING

Redemption is a present possession: "In whom we *have* redemption . . ." (Eph. 1:7). Redemption is ours here and now, this very moment. We have redemption because we have the Redeemer — *Christ*.

Our redemption is through the Redeemer, Christ Jesus:

"For I know that my Redeemer liveth, and that He shall stand at the latter day upon the earth . . ." (Job 19:25).

Our redemption is through the blood of Christ: "Forasmuch as ye know that ye were not redeemed with corruptible things, as silver and gold, from your vain conversation received by tradition from your fathers; BUT WITH THE PRECIOUS BLOOD OF CHRIST, as of a lamb without blemish and without spot" (I Pet. 1:18, 19).

Our redemption is not only for time, but for eternity: "Neither by the blood of goats and calves, BUT BY HIS OWN BLOOD He entered in once into the holy place, having obtained eternal redemption for us" (Heb. 9:12).

Because we are redeemed by the Redeemer, there are things from which we know we have been redeemed:

We are redeemed from all iniquity: "Who gave Himself for us, that He might redeem us *from all iniquity,* and purify unto Himself a peculiar people, zealous of good works" (Titus 2:14).

We are redeemed from the curse: "Christ hath redeemed us *from the curse of the law,* being made a curse for us: for it is written, Cursed is every one that hangeth on a tree" (Gal. 3:13).

We are redeemed from bondage: ". . . To redeem them that were under the law, that we might receive the adoption of sons" (Gal. 4:5).

The glorious day is coming when our redemption will be complete. We are redeemed spirit and soul NOW, but our bodies will be redeemed: "For we know that the whole creation groaneth and travaileth in pain together until now. And not only they, but ourselves also, which have the firstfruits of the Spirit, even we ourselves groan within ourselves, waiting for the adoption, to wit, the redemption of our body" (Rom. 8:22, 23).

"Redeemed! How I love to proclaim it!
Redeemed by the blood of the Lamb;
Redeemed through His infinite mercy,
His child, and forever, I am!
Redeemed, redeemed, redeemed by the blood of the
    Lamb;
Redeemed, redeemed, His child, and forever, I am!"

CHRIST OUR ADVOCATE

CHRIST OUR ADVOCATE

IF WE SAY THAT WE HAVE NO SIN, WE DECEIVE OURSELVES, AND the truth is not in us. If we confess our sins, He is faithful and just to forgive us our sins, and to cleanse us from all unrighteousness. If we say that we have not sinned, we make Him a liar, and His Word is not in us. My little children, these things write I unto you, that ye sin not. And if any man sin, we have an Advocate with the Father, Jesus Christ the righteous: And He is the propitiation for our sins: and not for our's only, but also for the sins of the whole world" (I John 1:8-2:2).

Concerning the advocacy of Christ we are entirely indebted to the First Epistle of John. There are many shadows and figures in the New Testament having to do with the *subject* of Christ's advocacy, but we do not find a direct statement on it any other place in the Bible.

Paul speaks of Christ's being at the right hand of God making intercession for us (Heb. 7:25; Rom. 8:24), and "intercession" in a sense covers not only the *priesthood* of Jesus, but

His advocacy as well. Paul does not directly mention Christ as our Advocate, although in I Timothy 2:5 he does tell us that Christ is the only Mediator between God and men.

The subject of Christ as our Advocate occupies far less space in the Scriptures than does that of His priesthood, and yet it is one of the most *important* subjects to the believer; *for the advocacy of Christ is the provision that God the Father, in His grace, has made for our sins after we are born again.*

The First Epistle of John was written to the heavenly family, the "little children" of God — heirs of God and joint-heirs with Jesus Christ. The key to this little book is found in chapter 1, verse 4: "*And these things write we unto you, that your joy may be full.*" This is God's love-letter to believers. Notice how it begins:

"That which was from the beginning, which we have heard, which we have seen with our eyes, which we have looked upon, and our hands have handled, of the Word of life; (For the life was manifested, and we have seen it, and bear witness, and shew unto you that eternal life, which was with the Father, and was manifested unto us;) That which we have seen and heard declare we unto you, that ye also may have fellowship with us: and truly our fellowship is with the Father, and with His Son Jesus Christ. And these things write we unto you, that your joy may be full.

"This then is the message which we have heard of Him, and declare unto you, that God is light, and in Him is no darkness at all. If we say that we have fellowship with Him, and walk in darkness, we lie, and do not the truth: But if we walk in the light, as He is in the light, we have fellowship one with another, and the blood of Jesus Christ His Son cleanseth us from all sin" (I John 1:1-7).

Then it is that John says, "If we say that we *have* no sin we deceive ourselves." He goes on to say that believers should *confess* their sins, and that Christ our Advocate is faithful and just to forgive our sins and cleanse us from all unrighteousness.

Through the inspiration of the Holy Ghost, John assures us that he knows what he is talking about: *He is speaking of the Incarnate Christ* — God in flesh — that which was from the beginning. John said, "We have heard, we have seen, we have handled THE WORD OF LIFE." (And of course *"in the beginning was the Word,* and the Word was with God and the Word was God . . . and the Word was made flesh, and dwelt among us.")

John points out, "This then is the message which we have heard of Him" — and the message is spelled out very carefully here: "GOD IS LIGHT, AND IN HIM IS NO DARKNESS AT ALL." He then goes on to explain that if we *say* we have fellowship with God, and yet walk in darkness, we are living a lie and do not know the truth. But if we walk in the light as HE is in the light, we fellowship one with another and the blood of Jesus Christ God's Son cleanses us from all sin.

I am so happy that the blood of Jesus Christ does not redeem us — and then cease to operate on behalf of our eternal salvation. We are redeemed through the blood. ". . . We have redemption through His blood, even the forgiveness of sins" (Col. 1:14). The blood redeems, but it does not stop there; it also *"cleanses us from all sin."* This is progressive. We are not only *cleansed* (past tense) when we are saved, but the blood *continues to cleanse* day by day as we walk with Jesus through this life.

TWO CLASSES

In I John 1:6 and 7 we see two classes of people contrasted — those who "walk in darkness," and those who "walk in the light."

The first group is composed of unsaved people, those who have no fellowship with God. Whatever they claim, whatever they pretend, regardless of church affiliation or outward show they are not saved, for God is light, not twilight. God is blazing, Shekinah glory — and in Him is no trace of darkness.

The second group embraces those who received the message God gave to John and the other apostles, and which they in turn preached — the message concerning "that eternal life, which was with the Father, and was manifested unto us." And since these had *received* the message they had been brought into fellowship with those who had preached the message to them, whose fellowship was with God the Father and with His Son, Jesus Christ, Saviour and Lord.

The group walking in the light are therefore children of God — children of God because they heard the message concerning the eternal life that is ours in Christ, apart from whom there is neither life NOR light. Those who do not possess Jesus by faith are walking in darkness, children of night. But we who have *received* Jesus have received both life and light: *We are children of the day.*

If we are saved by God's grace through faith in Jesus Christ, we fellowship with God the Father IN Jesus Christ — we "walk in the light as HE is in the light." Our position as believers is IN the light. We have fellowship with God the Father, and we have fellowship one with another. It is only in fellowship with God the Father and God the Son that believers can possibly have fellowship with one another here on earth.

THE NATURE OF THE ADVOCACY OF CHRIST

". . . If we walk in the light, as HE is in the light, we have fellowship one with another, and the blood of Jesus Christ, His Son, cleanseth us from all sin" (I John 1:7).

The last clause in this tremendous verse must be understood if we hope to understand the nature of the advocacy of Christ. This statement does not mean that the blood of Christ is being *constantly applied*. It does not mean that the

blood redeems us and washes our sins away, and then if we
sin afterward, the blood must again be applied, and this must
continue over and over and over again as many times as we
sin, until we are safe in heaven. If this were true, if God must
of necessity be continually applying the blood each time a believer sins, then there would be no need for Christ our Advocate.

When Jesus took the place of a servant, girded Himself
with a towel and bathed the disciples' feet, Peter refused to
let the Lord **wash** *his* feet; but Jesus rebuked him, and told
him, "He that is *washed* needeth not save to wash his feet . . ."
(John 13:10). The Greek words here translated "wash" are
not the same. The first one is "bathed," and the second is
"wash." The picture here is the cleansing of the blood, and
when once we are redeemed by the blood we do not need to
be redeemed (*bathed* in the blood) every time we sin; we
need *forgiveness* which our Advocate is in a position to grant.
The Holy Spirit declares through Paul, ". . . *By one offering
HE HATH PERFECTED FOREVER them that are sanctified*" (Heb. 10:14).

It is a cardinal truth of Christianity, a fundamental of the
true faith, that when the sinner believes on the Lord Jesus
Christ and puts his faith in the shed blood; when through faith
he is brought under the power and efficacy of the blood of
Christ, that sinner is cleansed from guilt through the one offering and *perfected forever* because of the blood. Consequently,
once bathed *in* the blood and redeemed *by* the blood, there
can be no *second application* of the blood. Chapters 9 and
10 of Hebrews declare this truth, and it will do you much good
to carefully study those two chapters. Feed upon them, hide
them in your heart.

"Christ is not entered into the holy places made with
hands, which are the figures of the true; but into heaven itself, now to appear in the presence of God for us: Nor yet
that He should offer Himself often, as the high priest entereth

into the holy place every year with blood of others; for then **must He often have suffered since the foundation of the world: but** now once in the end of the world hath He appeared **to put away sin by the sacrifice of Himself**" (Heb. 9:24-26).

Here we have the sacrifices of the old covenant which were repeated often — many times the same sacrifice for the same sin — set in contrast to the *one* sacrifice of the Lamb of God — God's Christ. The former was temporary efficacy; but the last offering, the one sacrifice of the Lamb of God, is *everlasting*. The believer who has trusted in the finished work of Jesus, believing that His shed blood cleanses from all sin, has his sins forever removed from the sight of a holy God. The efficacy of the blood of Christ is the answer: ". . . *Christ was once offered to bear the sins of many* . . ." (Heb. 9:28). God accepted the one sacrifice offered by His Son — His own precious blood, and that one sacrifice satisfied God the Father.

Jesus came into this world to bear the sins of many, and though "all we like sheep have gone astray," Jehovah God laid on HIM the iniquity of us all. Jesus bore our sins in His own body on the cross, the consequence being that the sins of those who are under the efficacy of His blood are forever gone from the sight of God. God cannot and does not see the sin that is covered by the blood.

In Hebrews 10 we find proof upon proof that there is *no more remembrance* on the part of God of the sins of those who are trusting in the finished work of Jesus and the shed blood of His cross. The believer has no more conscience of sins since he has been perfected forever by the one offering of Jesus Christ.

(In Hebrews 9:24-26 we have the contrast between the repeated sacrifices of the old covenant and the ONE sacrifice of the new — *Jesus the Lamb;* the former, *temporary;* the latter, *everlasting*, never to be repeated. Consequently those who are *under* the blood are *protected BY the blood*. Therefore, those who are under the efficacy of the blood of Christ know their sins are forever gone from the sight of God. But God removes the guilt of sin *ONLY on the MERIT of the blood of the Lamb.*)

It is absolutely essential that believers be clear on this point, for it stands at the very top of the list of the fundamentals of our faith. John does not speak here of the *application* of the shed blood of Jesus Christ, but of the *efficacy* of the blood. The blood of Jesus was not the blood of a man, but the blood of God: "Take heed therefore unto yourselves, and to all the flock, over the which the Holy Ghost hath made you overseers, to feed the Church of God, WHICH HE HATH PURCHASED WITH HIS OWN BLOOD" (Acts 20:28).

The characteristic of the blood is to cleanse from ALL sin — it has this power, this potency, this efficacy, this quality. May we use a very crude illustration here? We say, "That is *poison*. It will kill you." Thus we infer that the very nature of poison is to kill — it has the power to kill. *In the same way, the shed blood of Christ has the power to cleanse from all sin.*

This is a truth too wonderful for my finite mind to grasp. I cannot fathom the depth nor the height of it, nor the length nor the breadth of it! But if we believe the Word of God we must confess that those of us who are born again, washed in the blood, are *"in the light as HE is in the light."* We are prone to ask, "Is it possible?" And yet — why should we ask? We should say, "It is in God's Word and God cannot lie. Therefore *I believe it,* even though I cannot *understand it!*"

Dear brother, dear sister in Christ, can YOU take it in? Those of us who are covered by the blood are at this very moment in the light as HE is in the light! (And if we are NOT in the light as He is in the light, then we are not saved — because God is light and there is no trace of darkness in Him.) If we are saved our lives are "hid with Christ in God" (Col. 3:3).

Certainly we must face the fact that we are in the flesh

insofar as our Adamic nature is concerned, "Wherefore let him that thinketh he standeth take heed lest he fall" (I Cor. 10:12). We must face the fact that we are defiled insofar as falling short of the glory of God is concerned. As long as we are in the flesh we will be weak and unworthy and faults will be ever with us. We may be guilty of the sin of commission by doing things that are not right, or of the sin of omission by leaving undone those things which we ought to do.

We must therefore be always conscious of the defilements which we may daily contract in contact with things of this life — and if we should look at ourselves only through our own eyes we would throw up our hands in defeat! But we must bear in mind always that our fitness to enter heaven is wholly due to the cleansing efficacy of the blood of the Lamb of God — the Lord Jesus Christ who did no sin and in whom was no guile. He could say, *"For I do always those things that please Him"* (John 8:29), and in John 17:4 He said to the heavenly Father, "I have glorified thee on the earth: *I have FINISHED the work which thou gavest me to do."*

God the Father accepted the one sacrifice offered by God the Son. He received the shed blood, and that blood satisfied the righteousness and holiness of God. The sacrifice of Jesus satisfied every command and demand of a holy God; and the cleansing blood is ever there before the eyes of Almighty God — there to answer every claim that might or could be made against believers.

From the time of Adam's sin through the consummation of all things, it will always be with God the Father, *"WHEN I SEE THE BLOOD, I will pass over you!"*

GOD'S PROVISION FOR SINS COMMITTED BY THE BELIEVER

There are those who say, "I believe Jesus died to save sinners, and I believe He would save ME if I would call on

His name and ask Him to forgive my sins. I believe I could be saved, but I could not live the Christian life. I believe I could be saved, but I know I could not live up to Christian standards."

There are many who make this sad confession and entertain this erroneous idea about being a Christian. Sinner friend, God has not only made provision for your *salvation* —He has also made provision for any and all sins that may be committed by the child of God after conversion!

"If we say *we have no sin,* we deceive ourselves, and the truth is not in us" (I John 1:8). Notice the personal pronouns in that verse. John the beloved disciple penned these words which were dictated to Him by the Holy Spirit. He says *"we,"* and that takes in himself. *"If WE say WE have no sin, WE deceive OURSELVES and the truth is not in US."* John puts himself in this verse in five places, thereby actually testifying that if he should say he had no sin, he would be deceived and the truth would not be in him.

Since Jesus IS the Truth, and since when we know the Truth the Truth shall make us free, if the Truth is not in us we are certainly *not saved!* We dare not say that we have not sinned for *"if we say that we have not sinned, we make Him (God) a liar, and His Word is not in us"* (I John 1:10).

God has made provision for sin (singular) and for sins (plural). It is SIN (singular) that damns the soul: "He that believeth on Him is not condemned: but *he that believeth not is condemned already, because he hath not believed in the name of the only begotten Son of God"* (John 3:18). The sin of unbelief is sin enough to damn all the souls that have ever been born. All one need do to be eternally damned in the lake of fire is to *refuse to believe* on the Lord Jesus Christ. This is the sin that damns the soul.

But SINS (plural) rob the Christian of joy, power, influence — and yes, even of eternal reward.

In I John 2:1, 2 we read, "MY LITTLE CHILDREN" —
(This could *not* be directed to unbelievers, because it is ad-
dressed to the "little children" of God.) "These things write
I unto you, that ye sin not." (It is not necessary or imperative
that the child of God sin.)" And *IF any man sin,* we have
an Advocate with the Father, Jesus Christ the righteous: And
He is the propitiation for our sins: and not for our's only,
but also for the sins of the whole world."

This is the only place in the entire Bible where the term
"Advocate" is applied to the Lord Jesus, although in John
14:16 Jesus applies the term to the Holy Ghost when He
says, "I will pray the Father and He shall give you another
Comforter." The Greek word here translated Comforter is
the same as that translated "Advocate" in I John 2:1. In both
places the Greek word means *paraclete,* and Greek authorities
tell us that this word is extremely difficult to translate and still
preserve its full significance.

Vine's *Dictionary of New Testament Words* gives this
definition: *"Advocate* — literally called to one's side, i.e., to
one's aid, is primarily a verbal adjective and suggests the
capability or adaptability for giving aid. It was used in a
court of justice to denote a legal assistant, counsel for defense,
an advocate; then generally, one who pleads another's cause,
an intercessor."

"Advocate" is the best word that could be used, for it
sets forth the divine fact that Christ is seated at the right hand
of God the Father, and is in charge of our interests. Christ
is intrusted with our cause, He is at God's right hand as THE
ONE who has assumed the conduct of our case. He is there
to plead for us and to maintain communion between us and the
heavenly Father. So — if and when we sin, Christ pleads for
us as a lawyer in the courtroom pleads for his clients. He
secures forgiveness for us, thus maintaining communion and
peace between the believer and the heavenly Father.

Dearly beloved, believers deal — not with God the Father — but with *Christ the Mediator, the Advocate.* HE pleads our case. We confess our sins to HIM, and He is faithful and just to forgive us and cleanse us from all unrighteousness.

Christ, who is now seated at the right hand of God (Heb. 1:1-3) is our paraclete (Advocate) on high, while the Holy Ghost who abides within the bosom of every born again believer is our paraclete (Comforter) while we are here on earth. Christ is intrusted with our interest in heaven; the Holy Ghost is in charge of our interests here on earth.

". . . As many as are led by the Spirit of God, they are the (children) of God" (Rom. 8:14). The Holy Ghost indwells every believer, and leads us "in the paths of righteousness for His name's sake" (Psalm 23:3). If it were left up to us, to live a spiritual life in these bodies of flesh, we would find it utterly impossible to do so: "For the flesh lusteth against the Spirit, and the Spirit against the flesh: and these are contrary the one to the other; so that ye cannot do the things that ye would" (Gal. 5:17).

Thus the flesh and the Spirit are continually in warfare — but thank God, *"Greater is He that is in you than He that is in the world!"* We are more than conquerors, because the Holy Ghost leads us into the paths of right living, He leads us around the pitfalls of the devil and guides us in the straight and narrow way.

Dear beloved fellow believer, our heavenly interest is in good hands — Christ's hands; and our earthly interest and sojourn are in good hands — the hands of the Holy Ghost — and praise God, we are SEALED by the Holy Ghost until the day of redemption (Eph. 4:30). Rejoice and be glad — for He who has begun a good work in you is able to perform it until that glorious day — the day of the resurrection when we will be glorified with Him! (Phil. 1:6).

CHRIST AS OUR ADVOCATE —
CHRIST AS OUR HIGH PRIEST

The difference between advocacy and priesthood is two-fold. The Priest is *with* God. The foundation of His priest-hood lies in the one sacrifice which He has offered (Heb. 1:3; 7:27; 9:12). His intercession, therefore, as the Priest is based upon the everlasting virtue and efficacy of that one oblation which He offered on the cross.

Christ is before God in our behalf. Through His finished work on the cross we have access into God's presence, to enter the holiest by the blood of Jesus and to be inside the rent veil as worshippers (Heb. 10:19-22); and it is for us as such that Christ carries on the office of priesthood. We approach God through the Priest on the ground that our sins have forever been put away.

"So also Christ glorified not Himself to be made an high priest; but He that said unto Him, Thou art my Son, to day have I begotten thee. As He saith also in another place, Thou art a priest for ever after the order of Melchisedec. Who in the days of His flesh, when He had offered up prayers and supplications with strong crying and tears unto Him that was able to save Him from death, and was heard in that He feared; Though He were a Son, yet learned He obedience by the things which He suffered; and being made perfect, He be-came the author of eternal salvation unto all them that obey Him; Called of God an high priest after the order of Melchise-dec" (Heb. 5:5-10).

Christ is forever priest with God, and as priest he keeps the believer in perfect rest and peace through mercy and grace.

"Seeing then that we have a great high priest, that is passed into the heavens, Jesus the Son of God, let us hold fast our profession. For we have not an high priest which cannot be touched with the feeling of our infirmities; but was in all points tempted like as we are, yet without sin. Let us therefore come boldly unto the throne of grace, that we may obtain mercy, and find grace to help in time of need" (Heb. 4:14-16).

Jesus our High Priest keeps us in perfect peace and gives us rest when we are in trouble and have need. When we have heartaches and disappointments, we find in our High Priest grace to help in time of need. You will notice that *sin* is not mentioned in these verses except to state that Christ lived *without* sin, and since He lived without sin He is therefore qualified to act as our High Priest, and give us mercy and grace to help as we travel life's journey. It was not until AFTER He had purged our sins that He entered upon the functions and duties of His office as priest: " . . . When He had by Himself purged our sins, sat down on the right hand of the Majesty on high" (Heb. 1:3b).

We are children of God the Father by adoption. Christ through His shed blood purged our sins, saved us by His grace, imputed righteousness to us. Thus, because of our salvation through the finished work of Jesus, we were made fit to be adopted into God's family as children and to be placed in the position of "heirs of God and joint-heirs with Christ." We are sons of God *through the new birth,* children of the heavenly Father by adoption. Therefore, Jesus as our Advocate pleads to the Father as one would plead to an earthly Father in behalf of the child of that Father.

The qualification that makes Christ accepted as our Advocate is twofold:

1. *His Person* — who He was.

2. *His work* — what He did.

He came from the heavenly Father, and all that He did was to the glory of the Father. God was satisfied in every minute detail of everything Jesus did, everything He said, and everything He was. He IS the propitiation for our sins — and rightly so, because of the accomplishment of His shed blood on the basis of the efficacy of His blood. He is qualified, He has a perfect right to be the propitiation for sins committed by the children of the heavenly Father.

All hell could not destroy nor stop Jesus until He had forever cleared the sin-debt that stood between us and God the Father. He shed His blood for the remission of sin, and the blood He shed has been accepted by God the Father as full payment and complete atonement for all our guilt. On the merit of the shed blood, the work accomplished by Jesus our Saviour who is now Christ our Advocate seated at the right hand of the Majesty on high, His intercession for us can never falter nor fail. *He is JESUS CHRIST, the righteous.*

Christ is the ONLY one who has met the demands of each and every minute claim of God the Father, sovereign God from everlasting to everlasting. He met God's claims according to the standards of God's own immutable holiness. He glorified God the Father in every attribute of His being. Christ therefore is THE ONE who answers completely to the perfection and holiness of His own nature, having completely satisfied sovereign God who desires truth in the inward parts. God has found complete satisfaction in Christ — the Man who is now seated at His own right hand — the highest position in the high heaven.

Because of WHO He is and because of the WORK He did, Christ as our Advocate has an irresistible and undeniable claim upon God the Father. God could not remain God if He denied the plea of the Son of His love who met every demand of God's holiness and paid the sin-debt in full. Because of what Christ has accomplished, God's heart rejoices to hear and answer His intercession on behalf of believers who have sinned and come short of the glory of God. God the Father rejoices because now He can be righteous and holy and yet justify the ungodly on the merit of the finished work of Jesus Christ the Son:

"Being justified freely by His grace through the redemption that is in Christ Jesus: Whom God hath set forth to be a propitiation through faith in His blood, to declare His righteousness for the remission of sins that are past, through the forbearance of God; To declare, I say, at this time His righteousness: that He might be just, and the justifier of him which believeth in Jesus. Where is boasting then? It is excluded. By what law? of works? Nay: but by the law of faith. Therefore we conclude that a man is justified by faith without the deeds of the law" (Rom. 3:24-28).

TWO ASPECTS OF THE WORK OF CHRIST AS THE BELIEVER'S ADVOCATE

"If any man sin we have an Advocate with the Father, Jesus Christ the righteous" (I John 2:1).

We see here the aspect toward God. As our Advocate when we sin, Christ undertakes for us. He is our Intercessor, He is the One who pleads our case before God the Father on our behalf. It is not alone the *presence* of Christ that constitutes His advocacy, but also His activity in intercession for us when we fall into sin. To Peter Jesus said, "Simon, Simon, behold, Satan hath desired to have you, that he may sift you as wheat: BUT I HAVE PRAYED FOR THEE, that thy faith fail not . . ." (Luke 22:31, 32).

It is true that this occurred while Jesus was still here upon earth, but He is still praying for believers who are sifted and tempted by the same Satan who tempted Peter. In John 17:20 we read, "Neither pray I for these alone, *but for them also which shall believe on me through their word.*" Jesus prayed for you and for me while He was still here upon earth, and even now as He sits at the right hand of God He is still interceding on our behalf.

On the one hand, Christ's advocacy is toward the Father. He *actively* and *actually* pleads for us when we are in circumstances that call for His advocacy — *"if any man sin."*

On the other hand, His advocacy is ministry toward us, this phase of His advocacy being the *effect* of His intercession to the Father on our behalf.   John 13 sheds light on this aspect of Christ's office as Advocate; it records the *effect* of His advocacy toward the Father on our behalf, and in this passage is pointed out the *method of its application* to our individual need as a believer, as well as the *object* for which His advocacy is exercized.   In I John 2:1, 2 we have the advocacy itself.

Christ came into the world because God *so loved* the world.   God so loved that He gave the SON of His love. And JESUS loved — He came into the world and laid His life down for sinners.

The ministry of Christ flows from His own great heart of love.   Jesus looked upon the masses and was moved with deep compassion.   He saw them as sheep having no shepherd, scattered abroad (Matt. 9:36).   When He came in contact with those who were blind, He was always moved with compassion.   He wept over Jerusalem and said, "O Jerusalem, Jerusalem . . . how often would I have gathered thy children together, even as a hen gathereth her chickens under her wings, and ye would not!" (Matt. 23:37).

"Now before the feast of the Passover, when Jesus knew that His hour was come that He should depart out of this world unto the Father, having loved His own which were in the world, He loved them unto the end" (John 13:1).   This does not mean that He loved them up until the time of His death.   It does not mean that He loved them until the end of His earthly life and ministry.   It means that *God's love is perpetual* — He still loves, He will never *cease* to love, because He IS love.   Jesus came into the world because He loved us, He died for us because He loved us, He forgives

our sins because He loves us. As our Good Shepherd He goes with us all the way, even through the valley of the shadow of death, *because He loves us.* He sits at the right hand of God the Father to make intercession for us as our Advocate because He loves us. *His love is perpetual, it never changes.*

THE OBJECT OF CHRIST'S MINISTRY

"And supper being ended, the devil having now put into the heart of Judas Iscariot, Simon's son, to betray Him; Jesus knowing that the Father had given all things into His hands, and that He was come from God, and went to God; He riseth from supper, and laid aside His garments; and took a towel, and girded Himself" (John 13:2-4).

Here we find Jesus in fellowship with His disciples at the last supper — the Passover supper. He knew that His earthly sojourn was almost over and that His departure was near at hand. He knew, too, that His passing from this earthly life would carry Him to the right hand of the Majesty on high, to occupy that seat as Man: "For there is one God, and one Mediator between God and men, *the Man Christ Jesus*" (I Tim. 2:5).

Jesus knew that the Father had given all things into His hands. He had *come from* the Father and He would *return to* the Father. We see Him as He leaves the supper table after once more pointing out to the disciples that His time with them was about over:

"*He riseth from supper, and laid aside His garments; and took a towel, and girded Himself.*" (The towel is a symbol of service, the garment of a servant.) "After that He poureth water into a bason, and began to wash the disciples' feet, and to wipe them with the towel wherewith He was girded. Then cometh He to Simon Peter: and Peter saith unto Him, Lord, dost thou wash my feet? Jesus answered and said unto him, What I do thou knowest not now; but thou shalt know here-

after.   Peter saith unto Him, Thou shalt never wash my feet.
Jesus answered him, IF I WASH THEE NOT, THOU HAST
NO PART WITH ME" (John 13:5-8).

In this last statement we have the object of the act Jesus
performed as a servant washing the disciples' feet.   His departure from the supper table signified that He could no
longer continue with them in this world; and now, through
this act of service, He showed them how He would fit and
prepare them to have part with Him in the place to which
He was going: ". . . Truly our fellowship is with the Father,
and with His Son Jesus Christ" (I John 1:3).

In taking the place of a servant and performing a servant's
duties, the Lord taught His disciples how He would fit them
for and maintain them in this fellowship.   The object of the
foot-washing was to enable His children to have communion
with Himself and also with the Father in the place where He
was going.

On many occasions He had already told them that He
would return to His Father.   Now He was preparing them
for that moment when He *would* depart — but that did not
mean that fellowship with Himself would cease.   Fellowship
would be even greater — not only with Himself, but with the
Father also.

Peter at first refused to allow the Lord to wash *his* feet;
but Jesus said, *"If I wash thee not, thou hast no part with me."*
Peter answered, *"Lord, not my feet only, but also my hands
and my head!"*   Jesus replied, "He that is washed needeth
not save to wash His feet, but is clean every whit" (John
13:9, 10).   This statement from the lips of the Lord Jesus
Christ is the key that gives us understanding of the subject
here.

ONLY ONE CLEANSING NEEDED

The Lord taught Peter that there is no need of a second
cleansing — only the washing of the feet.   These men were

believers, followers of the Lord Jesus. *They had been washed* — and that washing could never be repeated. In the words of Jesus, they were "clean every whit."

This divine fact was prefigured at the consecration of the priest in the Old Testament era. Aaron and his sons were washed with water — a type of the new birth through the incorruptible seed, *The Word of God*. This happened before they were dressed in their priestly garments (Ex. 29:4). They went through the washing *one time* and it was never repeated, although a laver was provided for them to wash their hands and feet when they went into the tabernacle to perform their priestly service (Ex. 30:17-21).

This point cannot be stressed too strongly. *The believer is cleansed ONCE.* The cleansing of the *blood* is forever! When we are redeemed through the precious blood of the Lamb we receive forgiveness for sins (Col. 1:14) and we are "CLEAN EVERY WHIT." If this were not true, we would not be qualified to have access into the presence of God's holiness, for if one spot or wrinkle be found in us we could not enter inside the rent veil. But now, since Jesus has offered the one sacrifice — once, for all, for ever — all believers are invited to *enter boldly* into the holy of holies:

"Having therefore, brethren, boldness to enter into the holiest by the blood of Jesus, by a new and living way, which He hath consecrated for us, through the veil, that is to say, His flesh" (Heb. 10:19, 20).

But even though the disciples were "clean every whit," their feet would need *daily washing*. The feet point to the walk of the believer, and even though we are in a position of abiding acceptance before God (we have been "accepted in the Beloved" on the merit of His shed blood and His finished work), in our walk through this world we constantly contract defilement; and while this defilement cannot damage or destroy our standing before God as *sons of God*, we DO need to confess our sins and call on Christ to cleanse us from any and all defilement that comes about as we mix and mingle with the "tares" in this field where "the wheat and the tares" will grow together until the great Separation Day.

Sins committed after we are born again do not destroy our standing in Christ but they do destroy our communion and fellowship with Him, and with the Father. We must confess our sins and He, our Advocate, is faithful and just; He will forgive, and will cleanse us from all unrighteousness.

Someone may ask, "What kind of sins do believers commit? *How far in sin* will a believer go?" We do not have the sin-question spelled out as to how many, what kind, what size — if sin can be measured or graded as little, big, mediocre, or terrible. The only answer we have is in our present Scripture — the promise that if or when believers DO sin, we DO have an Advocate who is just and righteous, and He pleads our case to God the Father.

You may rest assured that if communion and fellowship are broken between a believer and Christ, the believer will know it. In the bosom of each believer God has placed a conscience that will immediately remind us when we have grieved the Holy Spirit and sinned against our Christ. Born again believers are keenly aware of those things in their lives which are displeasing to God; and if the Holy Spirit is allowed to search our hearts, if we will look into the mirror of God's Word, we will not be in darkness concerning sin. We have the light of the Word — a lamp unto our feet, a light unto our pathway. We can know — we WILL know — when we have committed that which grieves the Lord, or when we have left *undone* something He would have us do. Our God-given conscience will remind us, if we are truly born again.

Let us again turn our attention to the service rendered by Jesus when He washed the disciples' feet; When He left the supper table, His leaving denoted that He would shortly depart from their company and go to be with the Father. Everything that He did on that night is significant. For instance —

He poured water into a basin, and with that water He washed the disciples' feet.

We know that *water*, in the Scripture, is a symbol of the Word of God. Therefore, in the Lord Jesus washing the disciples' feet with water, we see the symbol of the water of the Word in action.

Jesus said to Nicodemus, ". . . Except a man be born of water and of the Spirit, he cannot enter into the kingdom of God" (John 3:5). The Spirit, of course, is the *Holy Spirit*, and the water is the Word. Scriptural proof? I Peter 1:23: "Being born again, not of corruptible seed, but of incorruptible, by the Word of God, which liveth and abideth for ever" (I Pet. 1:23).

James 1:18: "Of His own will begat He us with the word of truth, that we should be a kind of firstfruits of His creatures."

The water with which Jesus washed the disciples' feet was a symbol of the Word. The Psalmist asks, "Wherewithal shall a young man cleanse His way? BY TAKING HEED THERETO ACCORDING TO THY WORD" (Psalm 119:9).

In Ephesians 5:25, 26, speaking of the Church, Paul says, ". . . Christ also loved the Church, and gave Himself for it; that He might sanctify and cleanse it *with the washing of water by the Word.*"

Please notice that these Scriptures have to do with *cleansing* — the washing of the water by the Word. Writing to the believers in Ephesus, Paul admonished them to put on the whole armor of God, and *have their feet shod* with the preparation of the Gospel. In other words, they were to have their feet cleansed with the water of the Word, and then put on the shoes of the Gospel and walk in paths of righteousness, holiness, and purity (Eph. 6:11-17).

To the spiritually minded, it is evident that Jesus did not wash the disciples' feet just to set an example of humility. He did it to signify to them that after He returned to the

Father He would *still* be their servant in the office of Advocate; and even though they had been washed and were "every whit clean," their feet (their daily walk) would need cleansing often; and He would, as their Advocate, cleanse them through the Word.

BUT HOW? When we sin, the Lord Jesus Christ as our Advocate pleads our case with the Father — we might say He speaks to the Father in our behalf. The Holy Spirit troubles our hearts and brings us before the mirror of the Word of God. We *think* upon the Word, and the Word brings to memory the thing that God requires of us. And then, if what we have done or said is against the Lord and brings grief to His heart, the Holy Spirit convicts us, we confess our sins to Jesus Christ, and HE, our faithful and just Advocate, forgives us, restores us to fellowship, and removes the burden from our hearts. Thus we are washed and the contamination of sin is removed.

Do not confuse this contamination with that of the heart. It is NOT the inner man that is contaminated, but the *walk* of the believer:

"Whosoever abideth in Him sinneth not: whosoever sinneth hath not seen Him, neither known Him. Little children, let no man deceive you: he that doeth righteousness is righteous, even as He is righteous. He that committeth sin is of the devil; for the devil sinneth from the beginning. For this purpose the Son of God was manifested, that He might destroy the works of the devil. Whosoever is born of God doth not commit sin; for His seed remaineth in him: and he cannot sin, because he is born of God. In this the children of God are manifest, and the children of the devil: whosoever doeth not righteousness is not of God, neither he that loveth not his brother" (I John 3:6-10).

Luke gives us another beautiful picture of Christ as our Advocate, although this, too, happened during the Lord's earthly ministry:

When the enemies of Jesus arrested Him and led Him to the judgment hall, Peter followed "afar off." You are familiar with the story. He stopped outside the hall of justice with the enemies of Jesus and warmed himself by the devil's fire. Shortly, someone declared that Peter had been with Jesus — and Peter denied it. A bit later, the accusation was again made — and Peter denied it a second time. *The third time* he denied (with oaths) that he had ever even *known* Jesus. Just then the cock crew, and the Lord turned and looked at Peter. (Please note that Peter did not turn to look at Jesus, but *Jesus* turned to look at Peter.) "And Peter went out, and wept bitterly" (Luke 22:54-62).

So it is today. Jesus is now seated at the right hand of the Majesty — seated there as a Man, the Man Christ Jesus (I Tim. 2:5) — He who was tempted in all points as we are, yet without sin. And when we, His children, sin, He pleads our case as our Advocate. He is worthy, because HE DID NOT SIN.

There is a solemn, divine fact that needs to be emphasized here — a fact not understood by many believers. *No man can come to Jesus the Savior for salvation until God the Father draws that man*: "No man can come to me, except the Father which hath sent me draw him: and I will raise him up at the last day" (John 6:44).

All sinners would go to hell if God's HOLY GHOST did not arrest and draw them through His convicting power: "Nevertheless I tell you the truth: It is expedient for you that I go away; for I go not away, the Comforter will not come unto you; but if I depart, I will send Him unto you. And when He is come, He will reprove the world of sin, and of righteousness, and of judgment: Of sin, because they believe not on me; of righteousness, because I go to my Father, and ye see me no more; of judgment, because the prince of this world is judged" (John 16:7-11).

The same is true in the life of the believer. When Peter

denied the Lord the first time, he sinned — but he did not stop there. He denied Him a second time; and then, growing worse by the moment, he began to curse and swear as he denied his Lord the third time. And what was it that stopped his cursing and swearing? *Jesus turned and looked at him!*

So my dear believer, remember that if it were left up to you to save yourself you would spend eternity in hell — and even after you are saved, if it were up to you to *keep* your walk and your testimony clean, you would still end up in hell because nothing that defiles can enter the city of God. Were it not for the advocacy of Christ, were it not for the fact that when His children sin He reproves, convicts, and draws us, we would never *confess* our sins.

If Jesus Christ did not look our way *through the Word* and through the power of the Holy Ghost, and convict us when we have been disobedient and slothful in our Christian living, we would keep on going deeper and deeper into sin. So shout aloud, "BLESSED BE HIS NAME! HALLELUJAH! What a Saviour, who can take a poor, lost sinner, lift him from the miry clay and set him free! and then lead him in paths of righteousness until he is safely inside the Pearly Gates!"

The Lord Jesus Christ left the bosom of the Father and the glories of heaven and came to earth's sorrow with His eyes fixed on the cross. He went down under the billows of God's judicial wrath and paid the sin-debt in full. He satisfied the holiness of God that He might make propitiation for our sins and on that foundation be able to serve us as our Advocate with the Father throughout our earthly pilgrimage. He is worthy, He is able — and God the Father has accepted Him as our Advocate. What love! What grace! What mercy! And never forget that our repentance as a believer is the consequence of the activity of Christ as our Advocate with the Father.

NOW HEAR THIS

"So after He had washed their feet, and had taken His garments, and was set down again, He said unto them, Know ye what I have done to you? Ye call me Master and Lord: and ye say well; for so I am. If I then, your Lord and Master, have washed your feet; ye also ought to wash one another's feet. For I have given you an example, that ye should do as I have done to you. Verily, verily, I say unto you, The servant is no greater than his lord; neither he that is sent greater than he that sent him. If ye know these things, happy are ye if ye do them" (John 13:12-17).

If we rejoice because of the service of our Advocate on our behalf with the Father, we should never forget our own obligation — first to Him, and then to each other as brothers in Christ Jesus.

IN CLOSING

Christ is the believer's great Emancipator. He delivers us from the penalty of sin through His shed blood — His atoning death (I Pet. 2:24).

Christ delivers us from the power of sin daily by His risen power: "For whatsoever is born of God overcometh the world: and this is the victory that overcometh the world, even our faith" (I John 5:4).

Christ delivers us from the pollution of sin by His indwelling presence. Every believer is a possessor of divine nature (II Pet. 1:4; John 15:4, 5).

Believers are not paupers. Christ delivers us from the pauperism of sin by and through the riches of His grace; and the riches of His grace are past finding out (Eph. 2:7).

Christ delivers us from the pleasures of sin by giving us pleasures that the world does not know: ". . . In thy presence is fulness of joy; at thy right hand there are pleasures for evermore" (Psalm 16:11).

Christ delivers us from the principle of sin through His unknowable love and the operation of His great love in our hearts and lives (I John 3:6).

In the sweet by-and-by the Christ who saves and keeps us will deliver us from the very *presence* of sin in His glorious second coming (Phil. 3:20, 21).

There is nothing ordinary about our Christ. Everything about Him **is** superlative. His perfection is far beyond all question. Our Christ is the most powerful among the powerful, the mightiest among the holy and the holiest among the mighty. With His nail-pierced hands He has lifted empires off their hinges. With the same nail-pierced hands He has lifted prodigals out of the hog pen. Our superlative Christ has turned the stream of time into new channels. *He maketh all things new!*

Whatsoever He touches, whatsoever touches HIM, becomes new. Our Christ still governs the ages of ages, and when WE look up to God in prayer through our Advocate, the Lord Jesus Christ, we will always find *Him* looking down to listen to our petitions, and to provide for our every need.

The *love* of Christ is unknowable (Eph. 3:19).

The *riches* of Christ are unsearchable (Eph. 3:8).

The *joy* of our Christ is unspeakable (I Pet. 1:8).

The *ways* of our Christ are untrackable (Rom. 11:33).

The *grace* of Christ is inexhaustible (II Cor. 9:8).

The *peace* given by our Christ is unfathomable (Phil. 4:7).

Christ Himself is unsurpassable: "Who is like unto thee, O Lord, among the gods? Who is like thee, glorious in holiness, fearful in praises, doing wonders?" (Ex. 15:11).

Our Lord Jesus Christ is our hiding place. He is also our abiding place. Hiding in Christ is our guarantee of safety and peace. Abiding in Christ is our satisfaction. We do not need anything the world, the flesh, and the devil may have to offer. HE satisfies completely!

Jesus who died on the cross to save us, now as our Advocate sits at the right hand of God the Father and keeps us *for Himself* from the world — we are IN the world, but we are not OF the world. We are kept by His power.

Christ keeps us IN Himself from sin — we are in Christ, Christ is in US.

He keeps us BY Himself from Satan. We are in the yoke with Jesus, and Satan cannot snatch us away. We are yoked to our Keeper.

Christ keeps us WITH Himself for fellowship. He is Light, we walk in the light, and fellowship with Christ, with the Father, and with each other.

> *The penalty of sin is borne, the ransom for sin is paid,*
> *For all thy sins full satisfaction made!*
> *Strive not, dear believer, to do thyself what Christ has done,*
> *Claim the free gift, and make the joy thine own;*
> *No more by pangs of guilt and fear distressed.*
> *REST, SWEET REST!*

"Come unto me, all ye that labour and are heavy laden, and I will give you rest. Take my yoke upon you, and learn of me; for I am meek and lowly in heart: and ye shall find rest unto your souls. For my yoke is easy, and my burden is light" (Matt. 11:28-30).

CHRIST OUR
GREAT HIGH PRIEST

CHRIST OUR GREAT HIGH PRIEST

FOR EVERY HIGH PRIEST TAKEN FROM AMONG MEN IS ORDAINED for men in things pertaining to God, that he may offer both gifts and sacrifices for sins: Who can have compassion on the ignorant, and on them that are out of the way; for that he himself also is compassed with infirmity. And by reason hereof he ought, as for the people, so also for himself, to offer for sins. And no man taketh this honour unto himself, but he that is called of God, as was Aaron.

"So also Christ glorified not Himself to be made an high priest; but He that said unto Him, Thou art my Son, to day have I begotten thee. As He saith also in another place, Thou art a priest for ever after the order of Melchisedec. Who in the days of his flesh, when he had offered up prayers and supplications with strong crying and tears unto Him that was able to save Him from death, and was heard in that He feared; Though He were a Son, yet learned He obedience by the things which He suffered; and being made perfect, He became the author of eternal salvation unto all them that

97

obey Him; called of God an high priest after the order of Melchisedec" (Heb. 5:1-10).

"For when God made promise to Abraham, because He could swear by no greater, He sware by Himself, saying, Surely blessing I will bless thee, and multiplying I will multiply thee. And so, after he had patiently endured, he received the promise. For men verily swear by the greater: and an oath for confirmation is to them an end of all strife. Wherein God, willing more abundantly to shew unto the heirs of promise the immutability of His counsel, confirmed it by an oath: That by two immutable things in which it was impossible for God to lie, we might have a strong consolation, who have fled for refuge to lay hold upon the hope set before us: Which hope we have as an anchor of the soul, both sure and stedfast, and which entereth into that within the veil; Whither the forerunner is for us entered, even Jesus, made an high priest for ever after the order of Melchisedec" (Heb. 6:13-20).

It is true that Jesus is our Saviour. It is true that "Christ hath redeemed us from the curse of the law, being made a curse for us." But the Lord Jesus Christ is also *our High Priest* — a priesthood foreshadowed in many particulars in the Old Testament.

The priesthood of Aaron foreshadows Christ in a very striking way. In the consecration of Aaron, in one outstanding point Aaron is made to differ from his sons. Together Aaron and his sons were washed with water; and then apart from his sons, after putting the priestly garments upon Aaron, Moses poured the anointing oil upon his head to sanctify him:

"And he put upon him the coat, and girded him with the girdle, and clothed him with the robe, and put the ephod upon him, and he girded him with the curious girdle of the ephod, and bound it unto him therewith. And he put the breastplate upon him: also he put in the breastplate the Urim and the Thummim. And he put the mitre upon his head; also upon the mitre, even upon his forefront, did he put the golden plate, the holy crown; as the Lord commanded Moses. And Moses took the anointing oil, and anointed the tabernacle and all that was therein, and sanctified them. And he sprinkled thereof upon the altar seven times, and anointed the altar and all his vessels, both the laver and his foot, to sanctify them. And he poured of the anointing oil upon Aaron's head, and anointed him, to sanctify him" (Lev. 8:6-12).

We note that when Aaron was alone, not in the company of his sons, he was anointed before the sacrifices were slain (*without blood*); but later, along with his sons and in their presence, the sprinkling of the blood *preceded* the anointing with oil. Study Leviticus 8:13-30.

But *why*? What was the reason Aaron was anointed with oil *apart from the blood* when he was alone, and later, in the presence of his sons, he was anointed with the blood *preceding* the anointing with oil?

If we study and rightly divide the word of truth, the reason is evident: *Aaron with his sons* prefigures the New Testament Church, the body of Christ, as the priestly family; but Aaron *apart* from his sons — *alone* — is clearly a type of Christ. Thus, the anointing of Aaron without the blood sets forth the tremendous truth that his great anti-type was "harmless, undefiled, separate from sinners," and needed not therefore the sprinkling of the blood, seeing that He was clean, without spot or blemish, holy before God.

In one respect, Aaron could not possibly be as exact as the Christ whom he foreshadowed. Washed with water he was a *figure* of Christ's purity, but he could not, except in an official manner, prefigure the personal divine dignity of the Lord Jesus Christ.

Paul's letter to the Hebrew believers sets forth the divine truth concerning our great High Priest. In this epistle the Lord's priesthood is the main subject, and it is very significant that at the immediate outset of the epistle the Holy Spirit draws our attention to the dignity of the Person who is now our great High Priest:

"God, who at sundry times and in divers manners spake in time past unto the fathers by the prophets, hath in these last days spoken unto us by His Son. Whom (His Son) He hath appointed heir of all things, by whom also He made the worlds; Who being the brightness of His glory, and the express image of His Person, and upholding all things by the word of His power, when He had by Himself purged our sins, sat down on the right hand of the Majesty on high; being made so much better than the angels, as He hath by inheritance obtained a more excellent name than they" (Heb. 1:1-4).

God has spoken in these last days by His Son whom He has appointed Heir of all things, by whom Almighty God made the worlds — and where could we find enough adjectives or words to describe the beauty, the splendor, and the glory of the worlds? (When the Bible speaks of "worlds" it is not referring only to our earth. The reference also applies to the millions of stars, planets, and constellations through the innumerable billions of miles of outer space.)

The Son by whom God has spoken was the brightness of God's glory, the express image of God's Person. He is the One who at all times is upholding all things by the word of His power. He Himself purged our sins, and is now seated in the heavenlies at the right hand of Jehovah God. He was made so much better than the angels, He has obtained a more excellent name than they, and at His name every knee in heaven, in earth, and under the earth, should bow to the glory of God. *This* is our great High Priest.

This Person, our great High Priest, is GOD — yet He is man! Very God, very man. Therefore, when angels (or Moses, Joshua, Aaron or Melchisedec) are compared with Him they fade into insignificance and disappear like the fog in early morning when the sun breaks through. They are lost in His high, surpassing, eternal glory.

Most of us think of the WORK of the Lord Jesus Christ as our High Priest — and truly, it is profitable to study and learn all we can about His office, what He does for us as our great High Priest; but the first thing the Holy Spirit would have us recognize is *His Person* — the Person of Him who, as our High Priest, is now standing before a holy God in our stead. His qualifications, His ability and power to *execute* the office of our great High Priest depend entirely upon the character of His Person. Who *was* He? *Who is He now?*

He WAS in the beginning with God the Father. He was in the bosom of God, He was *very God.* But He took flesh, and in that flesh tabernacled among men. Had He not been very God and yet very man, He could not have made propitiation for the sins of unbelievers. Had He not been very *man,* as well as very God, He could not, through His death, have destroyed him that had the power of death, the devil. He took the flesh of man; He received His blood from God (Acts 20:28).

"But we see Jesus, who was made a little lower than the angels for the suffering of death, crowned with glory and honour; that He BY THE GRACE OF GOD should taste death for every man. . . Forasmuch then as the children are partakers of *flesh and blood,* He also Himself likewise *took part of the same; that through death He might destroy him that had the power of death, that is, the devil;* and deliver them who through fear of death were all their lifetime subject to bondage. For verily He took not on Him the nature of angels; but He took on Him the seed of Abraham.

"Wherefore in all things it behoved Him to be made like unto His brethren, that He might be a merciful and faithful high priest in things pertaining to God, to make reconciliation for the sins of the people. For in that He Himself hath suffered being tempted, He is able to succour them that are tempted" (Heb. 2:9, 14-18).

The *Person* of Christ gives security and assurance to His

office, and thus the Spirit of the living God gives assurance and comfort to our hearts by unfolding to the believer the distinctive glories and the singular dignities of the Person who fills the office of High Priest in our stead before a holy, righteous God.

The danger and deadliness of liberalism and modernism is that many men in the pulpits today talk about the wonderful MAN, the Lord Jesus. They say a lot of nice things about Him, but they stab Him in the back by stopping short of His incarnation. They preach that He was a *great man,* a great *leader,* a great *preacher,* the founder of a great *religion.* But Jesus did not come into the world to be a great teacher or healer, nor to found a religion. He came to lay His life down that poor, hell-deserving sinners might have life: "By the grace of God" *He tasted death for every man!*

FOR WHOM DOES THE LORD JESUS ACT AS GREAT HIGH PRIEST?

It is a Bible fact that Jesus came into the world to save sinners — ALL sinners who will come to God by Him. "Whosoever will," let him come. Whosoever shall call upon the name of the Lord shall be saved. Christ Jesus died for the sins of all sinners; He is the propitiation for "the sins of the whole world" (I John 2:2). It is also a Bible fact that He died to redeem all that Adam lost, and whosoever will come to Jesus for redemption, that individual He will redeem. He desires to be Lord of every believer. He IS High Priest of every believer, but *only* of believers.

There are those who teach and preach that He is the High Priest of all peoples, but this is not true. He is the High Priest of born again, blood washed believers only.

Anyone who studies the Old Testament should know better than to teach such error. Aaron executed the office of priest — not for all men, but for God's chosen people, Israel.

Aaron was the priest for those who had been brought into a definite and peculiar relationship with God, a relationship such as Israel held in the Old Testament era and up to the day when they rejected Jesus and the kingdom.

In the day of Aaron, the Israelites were the people of God on earth. Today, *believers* are the people of God on earth, the true Church. Therefore Christ fulfills the office of priest for born again, blood washed believers — and only for believers. But He did not take His seat at the right hand of the Majesty on high until AFTER "He had by Himself purged our sins" (Heb. 1:3). He is there to act as Priest in our stead since He has purged us from our sins with His own precious blood:

"For it became Him, for whom are all things, and by whom are all things, in bringing many sons unto glory, to make the captain of their salvation perfect through sufferings. For both He that sanctifieth and they who are sanctified are all of one: for which cause He is not ashamed to call them brethren" (Heb. 2:10, 11).

Here we clearly see that Christ is great High Priest for "the brethren" — those who are sons of God, sanctified, partakers of the heavenly calling, those who "come unto God by Him." He is great High Priest to all who are covered by the blood:

"Having therefore, brethren, boldness to enter into the holiest by the blood of Jesus, by a new and living way, which He hath consecrated for us, through the veil, that is to say, His flesh; and having an high Priest over the house of God" (Heb. 10:19-21).

WHAT ABOUT PRIESTS ON EARTH TODAY?

A mistake here can be fatal. Those who believe that there is anyone on earth today who can plead their case before God are deceived — with the most fatal deception possible. There is but ONE who can confess us to God (Matt. 10:32). There is but ONE who can mediate between God and man: *"For there is one God, and one Mediator between God and men, the man Christ Jesus"* (I Tim. 2:5). No minister, preacher, or priest on earth today can obtain forgiveness of sins on our behalf with God. The Word of God teaches no such doctrine.

Scriptural truth teaches that we do not go to a priest at all: We approach God *through OUR great High Priest, the Lord Jesus Christ,* on the grounds that our sins have already been put away, we have already been forgiven:

"For the law having a shadow of good things to come, and not the very image of the things, can never with those sacrifices which they offered year by year continually make the comers thereunto perfect. For then would they not have ceased to be offered? because that the worshippers once purged should have had no more conscience of sins. But in those sacrifices there is a remembrance again made of sins every year.

"For it is not possible that the blood of bulls and of goats should take away sins. Wherefore when He cometh into the world, He saith, Sacrifice and offering thou wouldest not, but a body hast thou prepared me: In burnt-offerings and sacrifices for sin thou hast had no pleasure. Then said I, Lo, I come (in the volume of the book it is written of me,) to do thy will, O God. Above when He said, Sacrifice and offering and burnt-offerings and offering for sin thou wouldest not, neither hadst pleasure therein; which are offered by the law.

"Then said He, Lo, I come to do thy will, O God. He taketh away the first, that He may establish the second. By the which will we are sanctified through the offering of the body of Jesus Christ once for all. And every priest standeth daily ministering and offering oftentimes the same sacrifices, which can never take away sins: But this man (Jesus), after

He had offered one sacrifice for sins for ever, sat down on the right hand of God; from henceforth expecting till His enemies be made His footstool. For by one offering He hath perfected for ever them that are sanctified" (Heb. 10:1-14).

Let me emphasize verses 12 and 14: "BUT THIS MAN, after He had offered ONE SACRIFICE FOR SINS FOR EVER, sat down on the right hand of God . . . For BY ONE OFFERING HE HATH PERFECTED FOR EVER THEM THAT ARE SANCTIFIED." (*"This man"* is none other than the Lord Jesus Christ, our great High Priest.)

But WHO is sanctified? The answer is found in verse 10: ". . . *WE are sanctified through the offering of the body of Jesus Christ once for all."* All who have received the shed blood — the death, burial, and resurrection of Jesus Christ — and have put their faith and trust in His finished work, are positionally sanctified. We are picked up out of the family of Satan and placed over into the family of God. We are set apart FOR God. Therefore, through the offering of this Man — one sacrifice, never to be repeated — "He hath perfected for ever them that are sanctified." How much better can one become than to be "perfected" by the one sacrifice of Jesus — our Saviour, Lord, and great High Priest?

CHRIST'S QUALIFICATIONS FOR OFFICE OF HIGH PRIEST

Earlier in the message I pointed out that had Christ not been very God and very man, He could not have qualified to be our High Priest, but there are other qualifications which are pointed out in this epistle to the Hebrews.

The first divine essential qualification for priesthood was *Divine appointment*: "And no man taketh this honour unto himself, but he that is called of God, as was Aaron" (Heb. 10:4). We know that Jesus was not self-appointed, He "glori-

fied not Himself to be made an high priest," but rather glorified the One who saith unto Him, "Thou art my Son, to day
have I begotten thee."

Also in Matthew 3:17, 17:2, and John 12:28 God the
Father spoke in an audible voice concerning the Son of His
love. Yes, Jesus meets the divine essential for priesthood —
He was God-appointed, God gave Him this honor and position. To know that our High Priest is appointed by God, to
know that this One through whom we approach God is *acceptable* to God, should bring assurance and comfort to the
heart of every born again believer.

The fact that Christ has been appointed to this office by
God the Father and now *sits at the right hand of God* destroys
forever the teaching and claim that there are human priests
on earth today. It is true that all born again people are "a
royal priesthood" (I Pet. 2:5, 9); but if any individual claims
to be a priest *on behalf of other believers,* that person is a
false priest. There are no scriptural grounds for any individual qualifying as a priest today. The priesthood is settled —
once, for all, forever, never to be changed or altered.

The Lord Jesus Christ is the last Priest to be appointed by
Jehovah God: "For those priests were made without an oath;
but this (Christ) with an oath by Him that said unto Him,
The Lord sware and will not repent, THOU ART A PRIEST
FOR EVER after the order of Melchisedec" (Heb. 7:21).

Three things are clearly pointed out here:

1. *Christ's personal glory*: He was the Son of God's love, the
only begotten of God, conceived of the Holy Ghost and born of
a virgin. His personal glory exceeds all others born of woman.
2. *His official glory*: Christ was a priest — not for a season or
until death — but *forever*. His priesthood is unending.
3. *The source* of Christ's office as High Priest was in the divine
will of Jehovah God.

HOWEVER

There is another qualification that must be pointed out, a qualification that Christ acquired while here on earth in a body of flesh: *Though a Son, He learned obedience "by the things which He suffered."* Even though He was very God in flesh, the only begotten and virgin-born Son of God, He lived here upon earth as man. He took a body of flesh in order to accomplish in flesh what the law could not accomplish because of the *weakness* of the flesh. It was a divine imperative that *as man* He suffer all of the bitter experiences, trials, and tribulations to which man is exposed here in this world of sorrow.

In Hebrews 2:18 and 4:15 we learn that Jesus suffered, being tempted in all points as we are, yet without sin. He suffered as no *mortal* has ever suffered. In the Garden of Gethsemane He personally met Satan and all hell had in the form of demons and spiritual rulers of wickedness. (I personally believe that Satan loosed against Him every demon hell afforded.)

When the devil was pressing the power of death upon the soul of the Lord Jesus Christ, and *in the spirit* Jesus went down into the very darkness and depth of death itself, as the consequence of such suffering and anguish, His pain and misery being so terrible and so great, His sweat became as blood! (Luke 22:44).

Christ as man in that dark hour drank the bitter cup to the last bitter dreg! In that hour, He was tempted as we are — yet without sin. In that hour of torment and suffering He learned by His own experience what the sinner must suffer in hell apart from the Saviour; and since He suffered such agony, being tempted, He is able to succor those who are tempted — *you and me.*

It may seem strange that the Bible declares Christ to have learned obedience by the things which He suffered; but we must remember that in the beginning *He was with God;* He was in the bosom of the Father. But He took a body, and in that body declared God to man; and He knew not what it was to obey until He took upon Himself the form of a servant. He humbled Himself, took a body of flesh like yours and mine, and *in the likeness of men,* being found "in fashion" AS a man, He became obedient unto death, even the death of the cross (Phil. 2:7, 8).

So whether we understand it or not, it is a Bible fact that Christ suffered all the agony and torment of an eternal hell that could be heaped upon a sinner. He suffered thus because it was a divine imperative that He learn obedience, that He might take our place fully, in every minute detail.

The one word that describes Christianity is OBEY. If we hear the Word of God and *obey the message,* we will automatically call upon the name of Jesus to save us. If we hear the Word of God and *obey,* we will automatically surrender to Him as Lord of our life. If we hear the Word of God and *obey,* we will recognize Christ as our High Priest, our Mediator, our Advocate — the only One who can stand between us and God's holiness!

Christ suffered all that He suffered in order to do God's will. The entire tenth chapter of Hebrews points out this divine fact. He pleased God perfectly in everything that He did. He did not falter or fail in any respect. He did according to the perfection of God's thoughts, and He did God's will perfectly in all things, even to the horrible death that He died.

Therefore, when in His agony and bitter sorrow He cried out to God the Father who was able to save Him from death, "He was heard in that He feared" (Heb. 5:7). Christ knew anguish of soul such as no man has ever known. We must remember that He was not in agony and sorrow for one person alone, but *for all the sins of all sinners of all ages.* God the Father responded to the prayer of Christ the Son because the Son had glorified the Father in perfect obedience.

Christ was the only person who ever lived upon this earth who *did* glorify God in perfect obedience — and *God demands perfection.* Nothing that defiles shall enter the Celestial City. All that enters there must be divine perfection.

CHRIST MADE PERFECTION

"And being made perfect, He became the author of eternal salvation . . ." (Heb. 5:9). How was the Son of God, very God in flesh, made perfect? Does the Word of God refer to *moral* perfection? Did Jesus need to be made perfect morally? Did He actually sin in the flesh? *NO! ! ! He did not sin, there was no guilt in Him.* Then what does the Bible mean by His being "made perfect"?

Hebrews 5:5-10 plainly tells us that Jesus learned obedience through the things He suffered. Thus, passing through the bitter sorrow and indescribable agony — and doing so IN OBEDIENCE TO GOD'S WILL — Christ the Son of God was *made perfect.* The perfection mentioned here is in relation to *qualification for the office of Priest of God,* and since through the things He suffered and the sorrow and agony He bore He was made perfect and qualified for this office, *HE BECAME "THE AUTHOR OF ETERNAL SALVATION UNTO ALL THEM THAT OBEY HIM."*

Before Jesus walked the last mile of the way to Calvary, He had a heart-to-heart talk with God the Father, as recorded in the seventeenth chapter of John's Gospel. He assured the Father that He had finished the work He had been sent into the world to do. He had glorified God and pleased Him in all things, and He had given man the words God had given to Him for that purpose. He had obeyed in every respect, in every detail, even to the drinking of the last bitter dregs of the cup that was so black and horrible that it terrified even the Son of God!

And since Jesus met all the qualifications laid down by

God's holiness; since He was qualified for the office of High Priest, God recognized Him as such and seated Him at the right hand of the Majesty — "an High Priest after the order of Melchisedec" — not for time, but for all eternity, never to be altered or replaced. Christ will be our High Priest until we are safe in the Pearly White City.

What a wonderful blessing, what unshakeable assurance, to know that we have a High Priest who can be touched with the feeling of our infirmities — One who was tempted in all points as we are, yet without sin; One who, on earth, experienced every heartache, agony, and suffering that we may be called upon to experience; One who is able to sympathize with us in our sorrows, disappointments, and weaknesses.

Our friends and loved ones may fail to understand us, we may be disappointed even in those who are nearest and dearest to us; but JESUS will never disappoint us! He has walked the same paths we walk, He knows every step of the way, He knows every pitfall and hindrance. He lived here and met life as we meet it — except that He never failed in any way. He knows how to present our case before God the Father. *I am so happy that there is a MAN in heaven who can intercede for us!*

OTHER QUALIFICATIONS

I would not close this part of the message without pointing out the effectiveness of the sacrifice Christ offered — the effective *virtue*, the indescribable *measure*, and the *potency* of that sacrifice.

"And they truly were many priests, because they were not suffered to continue by reason of death: But this Man, (Christ Jesus), because He continueth ever, hath an unchangeable priesthood . . . For such an high priest became us, who is holy, harmless, undefiled, separate from sinners, and made higher than the heavens; Who needeth not daily, as those high priests, to offer up sacrifice, first for His own sins, and then for the people's: for this He did once, when He offered up Himself" (Heb. 7:23-27 in part).

I would also like to point out that the one sacrifice Christ offered — the sacrifice of the new covenant — is far, far better than the multitude of sacrifices of the old covenant:

"For Christ is not entered into the holy places made with hands, which are the figures of the true; but into heaven itself, now to appear in the presence of God for us: Nor yet that He should offer Himself often, as the high priest entereth into the holy place every year with blood of others; For then must He often have suffered since the foundation of the world: but now once in the end of the world hath He appeared to put away sin by the sacrifice of Himself. And as it is appointed unto men once to die, but after this the judgment: So Christ was once offered to bear the sins of many; and unto them that look for Him shall He appear the second time without sin unto salvation" (Heb. 9:24-28).

In this tremendous passage we see the perpetuity of His priesthood — *it is unending.* We who believe on the Lord Jesus Christ for salvation can rest on the assurance that He is fully qualified and perfectly adapted to the office of our Great High Priest. We need not fear that He will fail us in the office He fills for us in the presence of God the Father.

WHAT IS CHRIST DOING FOR US NOW IN THE OFFICE OF PRIESTHOOD?

Jesus came into the world to save sinners. He willingly left the bosom of the Father, took a body of flesh, and in that body He died — *as Jesus of Nazareth.* He finished the work God gave Him to do on earth.

Now, *as God's Christ,* He is seated at the right hand of the Majesty on high. Therefore, His work at this moment is in heaven. The Holy Spirit is here on earth today, abiding in the bosom of every born again believer; but Christ our High Priest is in heaven, seated at the right hand of God: "Who being the brightness of His glory, and the express image of His Person, and upholding all things by the word of His power, when He had by Himself purged our sins, sat down on the right hand of the Majesty on high" (Heb. 1:3).

"Now of the things which we have spoken this is the sum: We have such an High Priest, who is set on the right hand of the throne of the Majesty in the heavens; A minister of the sanctuary, and of the true tabernacle, which the Lord pitched, and not man. . . For if He were on earth, He should not be a priest, seeing that there are priests that offer gifts according to the law" (Heb. 8:1-4 in part).

The Scriptures I have just given you show us beyond a shadow of doubt that Christ did *not* begin His priesthood until He had by Himself *purged our sins,* and had taken His seat at the right hand of the Majesty on high. We have noticed that He is a priest after the order of Melchisedec, "to whom also Abraham gave a tenth part of all; first being by interpretation King of righteousness, and after that also King of Salem, which is, King of peace" (Heb. 7:2).

When the Lord Jesus Christ returns to this earth with His saints after the Rapture, after the Tribulation period has run its course, then He will be "King of Righteousness," He will be the *true* King David, the *true* King Solomon, or *"King of Peace."* During the Millennium He will reign as King of Righteousness and King of Peace. During the Millennium He will fulfill the order of the priesthood symbolized by Melchizedec; but NOW, while He remains at the right hand of the Father, His priesthood corresponds to that of Aaron.

The foundation of Christ's priesthood is the one sacrifice which He offered; He *"by Himself"* purged our sins. The priests of the Old Testament offered up sacrifices daily, first for their own sins, then for the sins of the people. Unlike them, Christ did not need to offer up a sacrifice for His OWN sins, for He HAD no sin. *He was sinless.* Neither does He need to offer up sacrifices daily for the sins of the people, for He did this ONCE, when He offered Himself (Heb. 7:27). The sacrifice He offered was not the blood of goats, calves, or lambs; but "BY HIS OWN BLOOD HE ENTERED IN ONCE INTO THE HOLY PLACE, HAVING OBTAINED ETERNAL REDEMPTION FOR US" (Heb. 9:12).

Therefore, His intercession for us as our High Priest is based upon the eternal virtue and the eternal effect of the one sacrifice which He offered — His life, His blood — upon the cross. Jesus Christ the Son of God satisfied the sin-question, once, for all, forever. It will be a happy day in the lives of believers when we fully realize this. It is no longer the SIN-question; it is the SON-question: *"What think ye of Christ? Whose Son is He?"*

Jesus saves sinners through His shed blood. His priesthood has nothing to do with forgiving our sins unto salvation — (He settled *that* in His Person when He bore our sins in His own body on the cross.) God made Him to be sin for us (II Cor. 5:21). Now He is seated at the right hand of God the Father, the highest seat heaven affords; and He sits there as our great High Priest. Christ had *already paid the sin-debt,* He had already purged our sins, before He sat down on the right hand of the Majesty on high as our High Priest.

Christ made propitiation for our sins *before* He entered into the office of High Priest: "Wherefore in all things it behoved Him to be made like unto His brethren, that He might be a merciful and faithful high priest in things pertaining to God, to made reconciliation for the sins of the people" (Heb. 2:17). Before He entered into the Holy Place as our great High Priest, Christ through His shed blood obtained eternal redemption from sin for all who will believe.

Christ was once offered to bear the sins of many: "So

Christ was once offered to bear the sins of many; and unto them that look for Him shall He appear the second time without sin unto salvation" (Heb. 9:28). He bore the sins of many, He paid the sin-debt, and "whosoever shall call upon the name of the Lord," receiving His finished work, His shed blood, shall be saved, redeemed, and made a born son of God.

Through His shed blood, through the one offering He offered, He has perfected forever those who believe on Him. Their sins and iniquities are remembered against them no more. Study Hebrews 10:1-18. This Bible fact is one of the most important of the fundamental truths of Christianity. If an individual has put his faith in the shed blood of Jesus, he is covered by the blood and his sins are gone forever from God's view, on the grounds that Christ, God's own Son, willingly bore those sins and suffered for them. He was *the just One* who took the place of the *unjust* to bring us to God: "For Christ also hath once suffered for sins, the just for the unjust, that He might bring us to God, being put to death in the flesh, but quickened by the Spirit" (I Pet. 3:18).

Our sins are removed from us as far as the east is from the west. God has cast them into the depths of the sea, He has put them behind His back, and He remembers them against us no more. Through the precious blood of Jesus our sins are gone! They cannot be recalled or held against us, because God has forgiven us for Christ's sake. Before taking the seat of exaltation at the right hand of the Majesty as our High Priest, He humbled Himself to the very lowest and became obedient unto death, even the death of the cross, and He suffered all the misery and torment of an eternal hell that we, through His shed blood, might enter into the holiest (Heb. 10:19-22).

There is no place in the New Testament, there is no place in Christianity, for man-made, man-ordained, man-appointed priests. Jesus is our High Priest, and He is the only one who can take our place before God the Father.

CHRIST OUR REPRESENTATIVE BEFORE GOD

"For Christ is not entered into the holy places made with hands, which are the figures of the true; but into heaven itself, now to appear in the presence of God FOR US" (Heb. 9:24).

In the Old Testament era, Aaron was the representative of the people before God: "And thou shalt take two onyx stones and grave on them the names of the children of Israel: Six of their names on one stone, and the other six names of the rest on the other stone, according to their birth . . . And thou shalt put the two stones upon the shoulders of the ephod for stones of memorial unto the children of Israel: and Aaron shall bear their names before the Lord upon his two shoulders for a memorial . . . And the stones shall be with the names of the children of Israel . . . And Aaron shall bear the names of the children of Israel in the breastplace of judgment upon his heart, when he goeth in unto the holy place, for a memorial before the Lord continually" (Ex. 28:9-29 in part).

The breast is an emblem of love. The shoulders symbolize strength. Christ loved us so much He died for us, He loves us so much now that He upholds us before God the Father by His intercession on our behalf — and He has the ability and strength because of the effect of His shed blood. How wonderful to know that Jesus bears us before God upon His breast and upon His shoulders. He loves us, and *His strength* stands between us and God's holiness.

CHRIST OUR HELP IN TIME OF NEED

"Let us therefore come boldly unto the throne of grace, that we may obtain mercy, and find grace to help in time of need" (Heb. 4:16).

We are pilgrims on earth; our citizenship is in heaven; and this world through which we are traveling is a wilderness for believers. (Study Hebrews, chapters 3 and 4, in connection with the high priests and God's people in their wilderness journey.)

What the high priest did for Israel in the wilderness, Jesus is doing for us today in a much better way. We can travel with assurance and confidence because we know that we can come to the throne of grace, and, through Christ, obtain mercy and find needed grace to help in our time of need — *and His grace is sufficient.*

As we travel this pilgrim way, God has given us His Word — a lamp unto our feet and a light unto our pathway. God uses the Word to judge everything in our hearts that might cause us to step aside from the straight and narrow path of faith; He uses the Word to judge anything that might tempt us to seek rest and comfort in the desert of this world of sin and sorrow. Thus Paul speaks to us:

"Let us labor therefore to enter into that rest, lest any man fall after the same example of unbelief. For the Word of God is quick, and powerful, and sharper than any two-edged sword, piercing even to the dividing asunder of soul and spirit, and of the joints and marrow, and is a discerner of the thoughts and intents of the heart. Neither is there any creature that is not manifest in His sight: but all things are naked and opened unto the eyes of Him with whom we have to do" (Heb. 4:11-13).

Born again believers have a High Priest who has passed through the heavens as Aaron, the priest of God to the people of Israel, passed through the different parts of the tablernacle and performed the duties of a priest on behalf of the people. Our High Priest is Jesus, the Son of God. Our Priest is far, far better than the priesthood of Aaron, because OUR High Priest was tempted in all points as we are tempted, *yet He did no sin.* Therefore He can sympathize with our infirmities and our weaknesses. He knows that we are flesh.

Since we know that we *have* such an High Priest, one who Himself walked the same path we are walking, one who is touched with the feeling of our infirmities, believers are encouraged — yes, invited — to come boldly to the throne of grace to receive mercy and to help in time of need. He knows our every need; He is able and willing to supply those needs.

BELIEVERS INSIDE THE RENT VEIL

Born again believers have access into the very presence of Almighty God. We have access by virtue of the effect of the blood of Christ — and ONLY through His shed blood do we have access into God's holy presence. Christ is there at the right hand of God the Father as our High Priest, but in the true depth of spiritual things He is there *because of His shed blood* (Heb. 12:1, 2).

Jesus despised the shame of the cross, but He *endured* the cross because He saw the glory beyond. He therefore suffered unto blood, striving against sin, and through His blood He paid the ransom, purchased redemption, and today sits at the right hand of the Majesty on high as our High Priest. Because of His shed blood, and because He is at God's right hand today, *we have access into the very presence of God's holiness.* The believer's place is therefore *inside the rent veil,* not on the outside. We are there because of the one sacrifice which Jesus made, the sacrifice that put away our sins forever.

"Having therefore, brethren, boldness to enter into the holiest by the blood of Jesus, by a new and living way, which He hath consecrated for us, through the veil, that is to say, His flesh; and having an High Priest over the house of God; Let us draw near with a true heart in full assurance of faith, having our hearts sprinkled from an evil conscience, and our bodies washed with pure water" (Heb. 10:19-22).

THE UNRENT VEIL — THE RENT VEIL

Paul tells us in Hebrews 10:20 that the veil which hung before the most holy place in the tabernacle in the Old Testament era was a type of the flesh — that is, the humanity of Christ. He was very God, yet He took upon Himself the form of humanity. The veil was known as "the beautiful veil." It hung as a covering before the typical presence of God, the most holy place, separating the most holy place from the outer tabernacle or temple area.

Symbolically, Almighty God dwelt behind the veil. Shekinah glory danced on the mercy seat. The veil in the temple pointed to the humanity of Christ — God veiled in flesh. The veil in the temple shut men out from God. In the flesh, Jesus lived a beautiful life, a life of perfection; but the beautiful life He lived could never have saved us.

"Jesus, when He had cried again with a loud voice, yielded up the ghost. And, behold, the veil of the temple was rent in twain from the top to the bottom; and the earth did quake, and the rocks rent" (Matt. 27:50, 51). As Jesus hung on the cross, He could no doubt see the smoke from the altar in the temple and He knew that HE was the fulfillment of the sacrifice that was about to be offered there. Therefore He cried, "It is finished," and bowed His head and gave up the ghost, and as soon as the veil was rent in twain from top to bottom, the "beautiful veil" changed from a barrier between men and God into a gateway making it possible for men to enter into the very presence of God.

While Jesus walked here upon earth, His perfect life was a barrier between God and man. His perfection showed the exceeding sinfulness of man. He said, "Except a corn of wheat fall into the ground and die, it abideth alone: but if it die, it bringeth forth much fruit" (John 12:24).

". . . *It abideth alone."* In His humanity, before He laid His life down, Jesus abode alone; but the moment He died on the cross, through His death, burial, and resurrection the way was opened for men to become sons of God and receive life through Christ's death. Thus, through His death sons of God could *multiply.* It was a divine necessity that one die for the sins of the people, and if Jesus Christ had not died, His sinlessness as He walked upon the face of this earth could never have paid the ransom for our sins; but in His death, in His blood, He paid the ransom *in full.* He purchased redemption. It is because of His *perfect sacrifice,* the blood that He shed on the cross, that the way was opened for us into the very presence of God; and that way is now open *to all who will come unto God by Christ Jesus.*

In the olden days, under the old covenant, the High Priest must needs present the blood of the sacrifice, and the blood was the only plea he had by which to enter into the most holy place. So it is today: *He who would enter into the holiest* must enter by the blood of the Lamb! The blood of the cross is the only plea God will hear. But *through the blood of the cross of Jesus* we have an accepted sacrifice. God has accepted that sacrifice, and through His blood Jesus opened the veil that believers may enter with perfect assurance — yea, we are invited to enter *boldly* — into the very presence of God in the name of the shed blood of the Son of God.

THEREFORE

"By Him therefore let us offer the sacrifice of praise to God continually, that is, the fruit of our lips giving thanks to His name" (Heb. 13:15).

It is no wonder the Apostle Paul admonished the believers to "rejoice evermore and in everything give thanks, for this is the will of God in Christ Jesus concerning you." No wonder he said to the Romans, "We joy in God!"

By the way — how long has it been since YOU looked to God the Father and said, "Thank You, dear God, for sending Jesus! Thank You, God, that You set forth Jesus to be a propitiation through faith in His blood, that I might be saved from sin! Thank You for allowing me to be a servant of Your Son — and thank You so much for having exalted Jesus to the highest seat in heaven at Your right hand, as our great High Priest, as our respresentative before Your holiness!"

Never forget, "FOR GOD so loved the world, that He gave His only begotten Son, that whosoever believeth in Him should not perish, but have everlasting life" (John 3:16).

It was God who so loved us that He set forth Jesus and allowed Him to come into the world. It was God the Father who turned His head away from the Son and everything went black as Jesus cried out, "My God, My God! Why hast Thou forsaken me!"

Yes, Jesus suffered; but God also suffered. It is through God's grace (Heb. 2:9) that the love of God was brought down to us in Jesus; and Jesus declared God to man. Jesus who knew no sin was made to be sin for us, and the one sacrifice He offered — His life — satisfied God the Father and brought glory to Him. Therefore God accepted the one sacrifice of His Son, and now Jesus sits at the right hand of the Majesty on high to make intercession — for you, and for me.

To Israel God gave Moses, Aaron, and Joshua; but to you and me He has given His own beloved Son, the Lord Jesus Christ. He has given us heaven's brightest, heaven's most precious, the Pearl of great price, the most glorious One heaven afforded.

Since this is a Bible fact, how should this tremendous truth affect us? "Seeing then that we have a great High Priest, that is passed into the heavens, Jesus the Son of God, let us hold fast our profession" (Heb. 4:14).

"Let us hold fast the profession of our faith without wavering; for He is faithful that promised" (Heb. 10:23).

ASSURANCE FOR THE BELIEVER

Since Christ is our High Priest, since we know that He is now seated at the right hand of the Majesty because God accepted the one sacrifice (His shed blood), we have this assurance: "WHEREFORE HE IS ABLE to save to the uttermost them that come unto Cod by Him, SEEING HE EVER LIVETH TO MAKE INTERCESSION FOR THEM" (Heb. 7:25).

Just what does it mean to "save to the uttermost"? The Greek points out that He is able to save *completely*. He is able to save *all the way*, even to the valley of the shadow of death. He is able to save altogether, *nothing lacking* — complete salvation with no flaw, complete as only a holy God knows completeness and perfection.

Jesus died once, to die no more. He died for the sins of the whole wide world, but now He is alive *forever*. Christ has an unchangeable priesthood. He has this unchangeable priesthood on the merit of His finished work, His shed blood. He died to save us from our sins. He lives at the right hand of God the Father to plead our case, to stand in our stead before God's holiness. He will never let us down, He will never fail us. His intercession for us is uninterrupted and we have an absolute, divine guarantee that we shall not perish in the wilderness of sin; we will enter the rest God has provided for His own: *"There remaineth therefore a rest to the people of God"* (Heb. 4:9).

If you are a child of God through faith in the shed blood of Jesus the Saviour, press on, weary pilgrim, press on! Do not look upon things around you, but look to HIM, the author of eternal life. Look to HIM, the author and finisher of our faith. Look to Him who is our Saviour, Redeemer, Lord, Advocate, and High Priest.

Dear reader, if you are NOT a believer, hear the words of the Lord Jesus: "Come unto me, all ye that labour and are heavy laden, and I will give you rest. Take my yoke upon you, and learn of me: for I am meek and lowly in heart: and ye shall find rest unto your souls. For my yoke is easy, and my burden is light" (Matt. 11:28-30).

"Believe on the Lord Jesus Christ, and thou shalt be saved" (Acts 16:31).

"That if thou shalt confess with thy mouth the Lord Jesus, and shalt believe in thine heart that God hath raised Him from the dead, thou shalt be saved. For with the heart man believeth unto righteousness; and with the mouth confession is made unto salvation" (Rom. 10:9, 10).

CHRIST OUR LIFE

CHRIST OUR LIFE

T HE THIEF COMETH NOT but for to steal, to kill, and to destroy: I am come that they might have life, and that they might have it more abundantly" (John 10:10).

"Verily, verily, I say unto you, He that heareth my word, and believeth on Him that sent me, hath everlasting life, and shall not come into condemnation; but is passed from death unto life" (John 5:24).

"And this is the record, that God hath given to us eternal life, and this life is in His Son. He that hath the Son hath life; and he that hath not the Son of God hath not life. These things have I written unto you that believe on the name of the Son of God" (I John 5:11-13).

"In Him was life; and the life was the light of men. And the light shineth in darkness; and the darkness comprehended it not" (John 1:4, 5).

When the Lord Jesus left the Father's bosom and came into the world, He came into a world of darkness; darkness engulfed the peoples of earth — yea, the darkness of spiritual night, *the darkness of death,* prevailed throughout the whole earth.

Job describes the condition of this earth when Jesus came: "... *The land of darkness and the shadow of death; a land of darkness, as darkness itself; and of the shadow of death, without any order, and where the light is as darkness"* (Job 10:21, 22).

Writing to the believers in Rome, Paul said, "Wherefore, as by one man sin entered into the world, and death by sin; and so death passed upon all men, for that all have sinned" (Rom. 5:12).

A sad picture indeed! There was not one ray of light to penetrate the total darkness that engulfed man's condition. Through the disobedience of one man, sin, death, and darkness moved upon ALL men. Not only did sin and darkness reign in the *hearts* of men, but *Satan* reigned *over* man and held him in subjection.

Satan became *the prince of this world:* "Now is the judgment of this world: now shall the prince of this world be cast out" (John 12:31). But thanks be unto God who promised Adam in the Garden of Eden that the seed of the woman would bruise the head of the serpent: "And I will put enmity between thee and the woman, and between thy seed and her seed; it shall bruise thy head, and thou shalt bruise his heel" (Gen. 3:15). The promise made by God to Adam was fulfilled in God's due season:

"But when the fulness of the time was come, God sent forth His Son, made of a woman, made under the law" (Gal. 4:4).

"In the fulness of time" as appointed by Almighty God (who perfected salvation before ever He made the dust from which He formed Adam) *the seed of the woman came* — made under the law, to redeem, to save, to deliver. What the law could not do because it was weak through the flesh,

God did *in flesh in His Son,* for truly, Jesus was God in flesh (II Cor. 5:19).

"In the beginning was the Word, and the Word was with God, and the Word was God. The same was in the beginning with God. All things were made by Him, and without Him was not any thing made that was made" (John 1:1-3).

When Jesus stepped from the bosom of the Father to the manger in Bethlehem, He came into the world of darkness — but there was a difference the moment "the seed of the women" came into the dark world. All around Him was darkness — the darkness of sin, the darkness of death; but IN HIM was life, and the life in Him was light — yea, *"the light of men."* The light of the Lord Jesus and the darkness of Satan were thus in contact. The light of the Lord Jesus shone in the darkness of sin, and the darkness of sin comprehended it not.

He who brought light into this dark world is "the true Light which lighteth every man that cometh into the world" (John 1:9). It is sad but true that only a few received the Light, but the Light was shining for *everyone* and he who remained in the darkness of sin did so simply because he would not turn his face to the light of the Lord Jesus Christ.

The Lord Jesus, *the Light of the world,* "was in the world, and the world was made by Him, and the world knew Him not. He came unto His own, and His own received Him not. But as many as received Him, to them gave He power to become the sons of God, even to them that believe on His name: Which were born, not of blood, nor of the will of the flesh, nor of the will of man, but of God" (John 1:10-13).

Notice — *only those who received Him were illuminated.* Only those who received the Light were made light. Those who received the Word, (the entrance of the Word giveth light), being illuminated by the Light, received the life of God. They were "BORN OF GOD." It is God who does the "borning." We are not born of man, nor of blood, of flesh, nor of any power other than the power of God. He alone has the power to "born" us and put life within us. He alone can put life and light into a person who is engulfed by darkness and shackled by Satan.

"And this is the condemnation, that light is come into the world, and men loved darkness rather than light, because their deeds were evil. For every one that doeth evil hateth the light, neither cometh to the light, lest his deed should be reproved. But he that doeth truth cometh to the light, that his deeds may be made manifest, that they are wrought in God" (John 3:19-21).

CHRIST — THE LIFE OF GOD

Since Jesus was God in flesh, during His earthly sojourn He had life in Himself because He was the Son of God — God incarnate, conceived by the Holy Ghost; the Word in flesh. He was *the life of God in flesh,* and hence, "as the Father raiseth up the dead, and quickeneth them; even so the Son quickeneth whom He will" (John 5:21).

"For the life was manifested, and we have seen it, and bear witness, and shew unto you that eternal life, which was with the Father, and was manifested unto us" (I John 1:2).

Jesus was in the bosom of the Father. No man has seen God at any time. The only begotten Son "hath declared Him." Jesus was the Word in flesh. He came in flesh to make known God the Father, the Father of all light and life.

All who believe on Him have life. All who believe are quickened, made alive. In this marvelous day of grace we not only have life, but we have life "more abundantly," and this abundant life is made possible only through the death and the resurrection of the Lord Jesus Christ. In this present and marvelous Dispensation of Grace, abundant life is the fruit of His finished work. Before He died on the cross He said, "It is finished" (John 19:30).

Just before He went to Calvary He said, "Father, the hour is come; glorify thy Son, that thy Son also may glorify thee: As thou hast given Him power over all flesh, that He should give eternal life to as many as thou hast given Him" (John 17:1, 2).

CHRIST — THE PRINCE OF LIFE

On the Day of Pentecost, Peter preached one of the most powerful sermons ever delivered by the lips of man. He made known to Israel that Jesus of Nazareth whom they had crucified "hath God raised up, whereof we all are witnesses. Therefore being by the right hand of God exalted, and having received of the Father the promise of the Holy Ghost, He hath shed forth this, which ye now see and hear . . . Therefore let all the house of Israel know assuredly, that God hath made that same Jesus, whom ye have crucified, both Lord and Christ" (Acts 2:32-36 in part.

In his second sermon Peter said, "But ye denied the Holy One and the Just, and desired a murderer to be granted unto you; and killed *THE PRINCE OF LIFE*, whom God hath raised from the dead; whereof we are witnesses" (Acts 3:14, 15).

It was a divine imperative that Christ should die in order to become "the Prince of life."

". . . The wages of sin is death; but the gift of God is eternal life through Jesus Christ our Lord" (Rom. 6:23). God declared to Adam, "In the day thou eatest thereof, thou shalt surely die" (Gen. 2:17). In Adam ALL die, and hence, as long as the sin-question was not dealt with and God's righteous claims upon man were unmet and unsatisfied because of sin, it was only natural for death to continue to reign. And from the time the first Adam sinned until the time "the last Adam" (I Cor. 15:45) said, "It is finished" and literally laid His life down, death *did* continue to reign. But now death is a defeated foe.

Man brought death upon himself as the consequence and penalty of his sins. Adam did not sin in ignorance — he knew the penalty for disobeying God, but he deliberately disobeyed and stepped over God's command, doing what God had commanded him not to do.

Until there was One (the Lord Jesus Christ) who was qualified, willing, and able in the sight of a Holy God to take the case of sin and settle it with God according to God's holy demands, there was no hope for the sinner. From Eden to Calvary God passed over man's sins, but those sins were never taken away until the Lamb of God offered one sacrifice — once, for all, forever. We read in John 1:29, "BEHOLD THE LAMB OF GOD, WHICH TAKETH AWAY THE SIN OF THE WORLD!"

By His death the Lamb of God, the only begotten of the Father, met all of God's claims upon the sinner who deserved eternal death and damnation in the lake of fire. The Lamb of God went down under the wrath that was to be poured out upon the sinner — the sinner's righteous due. Jesus took the sinner's place and suffered all the agony, all the misery and woe of an eternal hell, that WE might be set free through faith in His finished work. Yes, Jesus who was dead is alive again! He lives forevermore.

The sin-question is settled in Hebrews 10: "For the law having a shadow of good things to come, and not the very image of the things, can never with those sacrifices which they offered year by year continually make the comers thereunto perfect. For then would they not have ceased to be offered? because that the worshippers once purged should have had no more conscience of sins. But in those sacrifices there is a remembrance again made of sins every year. For it is not possible that the blood of bulls and of goats should take away sins. Wherefore when He cometh into the world, He saith, Sacrifice and offering thou wouldest not, but a body hast thou prepared me: In burnt-offerings and sacrifices for sin thou hast had *no pleasure.* Then said I, Lo, I come (in the volume of the book it is written of me,) to do thy will, O God. Above when He said, Sacrifice and offering and burnt-offerings and offering for sin thou wouldest not, *neither hadst pleasure* therein; which are offered by the law; Then said He, Lo, I come to do thy will, O God. He taketh away the first, that He may establish the second. By the which will we are sanctified through the offering of the body of Jesus Christ once for all. And every priest standeth daily ministering and offering oftentimes the same sacrifices, *which can never take away sins:* BUT THIS MAN, after He had offered one sacrifice for sins for ever, sat down on the right hand of God; From henceforth expecting till His enemies be made His footstool. *FOR BY ONE OFFERING HE HATH PERFECTED FOR EVER THEM THAT ARE SANCTIFIED"* (Heb. 10:1-14).

If the Lamb of God had not gone to Calvary, if He had not shed His blood, every drop of blood shed from Adam to Calvary would have been in vain. The blood of lambs, doves, pigeons, bullocks, could not take away sins. It is not possible that the blood of these animals should take away sins. That blood simply stood before the blazing eyes of God's holiness — a shadow, a temporary covering; but the blood of Jesus Christ literally takes our sins away. Jesus bore our sins in His own body and nailed them to His cross. He was made sin for us that we, in Him, might be made the righteousness of God; and on the merit of HIS shed blood, God has made us *"accepted in the Beloved."* Apart from the shed blood of Jesus Christ there is no life eternal.

It is no longer the sin-question, but the SON-question. The question that will determine your eternal destiny is *"What think ye of Christ? Whose Son is He?"* Jesus Christ, the Son of God, settled the sin-question once, for all, forever, and all who believe on Him and put their trust in His shed blood receive life eternal.

Jesus made full and perfect atonement. The sacrifice He offered pleased and glorified God, and God has given Him the highest seat in heaven — the seat at the right hand of the Majesty. God placed His stamp of approval upon the finished work of Jesus when He raised Him from the dead and placed Him at the right hand of the Majesty on high. Now Jesus Christ the Lord is the living One. Death has no more dominion over Him. Since He was dead and is alive again — and behold, He lives forevermore — He CAN bestow eternal life upon all who come to Him.

"Therefore as by the offence (*singular — ONE offence*) judgment came upon all men to condemnation; even so by the righteousness of One (*singular — one righteousness*) the free gift came upon ALL men unto justification of life. For as by ONE MAN'S DISOBEDIENCE many were made sinners, so by THE OBEDIENCE OF ONE shall many be made righteous" (Rom. 5:18, 19).

God will not acquit the wicked (Nahum 1:3). It was God's holiness that demanded the death of Jesus Christ, and it was a divine imperative that He die AS He died — on the cruel cross. It was *only by God's grace* that Jesus was allowed to take the sinner's place (Heb. 2:9); and it is *only on the foundation of the finished work of Jesus* that God can now be righteous and yet justify the ungodly. On the merit of the finished work of Jesus, God can bring from the dead those who deserve eternal death in the lake of fire, and give them life when they believe on the Lord Jesus Christ and put their faith in His shed blood for the remission of sin.

There is no life eternal except in and through the Lord Jesus Christ: *"He that believeth on the Son hath everlasting life: and he that believeth not the Son shall not see life; BUT THE WRATH OF GOD ABIDETH ON HIM"* (John 3:36).

THE MEANS BY WHICH LIFE ETERNAL IS RECEIVED

Life eternal is received by faith alone. God's grace saves us, but faith exercised in the finished work of Jesus brings saving faith: "Verily, verily, I say unto you, He that heareth my word, and believeth on Him that sent me, hath everlasting life, and shall not come into condemnation; but is passed from death unto life" (John 5:24).

The Greek language here reads, "He that heareth my word, and believeth HIM that sent me. . ." (The preposition "on" does not appear in the original.) Abraham believed God — He did not simply believe that there IS a God — he BELIEVED God, and it was counted unto him for righteousness (Rom. 4:3).

John 5:24 puts the marvelous grace of God on display. We, dead in trespasses and sins, *reaping the wages of sin,* would have reaped eternal death had it not been for the grace of God allowing Jesus to die on the cross in our stead. But *because* of God's amazing grace and His rich mercy, because of His great love wherewith He loved us even when we were yet sinners, Christ died FOR us (Rom. 5:8).

We have all sinned. We have all come short of the glory of God. There is none righteous — no, not one. We have all gone astray. There is not a just man upon the earth that doeth good and sinneth not. But NOW, thank God, through the death of Jesus Christ, even though "the wages of sin is death," Jesus died to pay the sin-debt and we can have the gift of God (eternal life) through Jesus Christ, our Lord.

"All we like sheep have gone astray; we have turned every one to his own way; and the Lord (Jehovah) hath laid on Him (Jesus) the iniquity of us all" (Isa. 53:6). The sins and iniquities of ALL have been laid upon Jesus, He bore them to the cross and nailed them there. Therefore, the gift of

God through the Lord Jesus Christ is life eternal, and this gift is to all who receive Jesus.

The only way to receive Jesus is to hear the Word, and believe Him who sent Jesus. God has provided life eternal for all — life out of death. Through the death of the only begotten Son of God, life is made possible to all who will believe — and that life is God's free gift, it is not of works.

"And this is the record, that God hath given to us eternal life, and this life is in His Son. He that hath the Son hath life; and he that hath not the Son of God hath not life (I John 5:11, 12).

Please notice: *This is the record* — "He that heareth my Word." (The Word is the record, the record is the Word.) And the record is, "God the Father has given to us eternal life." We do not earn this life, we do not merit this life. But God GIVES us eternal life, and the life He gives IS IN HIS SON. There is no other place to find life. All else is death. Jesus is light and life, and "he who hath the Son hath life." He who does not have the Son does not have life, but abides in death — and when sin is full grown, *eternal death* in the lake of fire will be the wages received by the unbeliever.

Every believer has eternal life, but he should face the solemn fact that he is never said to have eternal life *in himself*. The eternal life of the believer is IN GOD'S SON, and the believer has eternal life because divine nature abides in our bosom when we are born again (II Pet. 1:4).

Jesus said, ". . . Except ye eat the flesh of the Son of man, and drink His blood, ye have no life in you" (John 6: 53). There were many who turned and went away from Him when they heard this saying. They said, "This is an hard saying; who can hear it?"

What DOES the Word mean when it declares, "Except you eat the flesh of the Son of man and drink His blood, you have no life in you"? The only place to find the right answer to a Bible question is in the Bible. (The best commentary ON the Bible is the Bible itself.)

In John 1:1 and 14 we read, "In the beginning was the Word, and the Word was with God, and the Word was God . . . And the Word was made flesh, and dwelt among us, (and we beheld His glory, the glory as of the only begotten of the Father,) full of grace and truth." Jesus was the Word wrapped up in flesh. He said, "The words I speak, they are spirit and they are life." So when we appropriate, assimilate, and take the Word of God into our hearts by faith, we are assimilating and appropriating the flesh and blood of the Son of man, because it is the Word that brings life, and Jesus WAS that Word, WRAPPED UP IN FLESH. We are saved by God's grace through faith, saving faith comes by hearing and hearing by the Word of God. We are born again — not of corruptible seed, but of seed that cannot corrupt — by the Word of God.

Jesus said, "Now ye are clean through the Word which I have spoken unto you" (John 15:3).

The entrance of the Word giveth light — and life; and this life is in God's Son. Eternal life therefore is only in Jesus Christ — "Christ in you, the hope of glory" (Col. 1:27).

LIFE IN JESUS

It is extremely important that we notice in the Word of God that eternal life is never said to be in ourselves, nor through anything that we ourselves can do, give, or possess. Eternal life is always "*in His Son.*" This divine and undeniable Bible fact guarantees absolute security to the truly bloodwashed, born again possessor of Jesus Christ. Whosoever would take away our eternal life must first pluck us out of Christ in God: "*For ye are dead, and your life is hid with Christ in God*" (Col. 3:3).

"Grieve not the Holy Spirit of God, whereby ye *are*

sealed unto the day of redemption" (Eph. 4:30). In Christ we are hidden in God, sealed by the Holy Ghost, and seated at the right hand of the Majesty on high, in the heavenlies in Christ Jesus (Eph. 2:6, 7). *CHRIST is our life.*

OUR LIFE — WHERE IS IT?

"For our conversation (citizenship) is in heaven; from whence also we look for the Saviour, the Lord Jesus Christ: who shall change our vile body, that it may be fashioned like unto His glorious body, according to the working whereby He is able even to subdue all things unto Himself" (Phil. 3:20, 21).

We are pilgrims in a strange land; our citizenship is in heaven. We are in the world, but we are not OF the world. We are dead to this world and alive unto God. We were dead in sins, we are now quickened together with Christ — by grace. We are saved NOW — and are made to sit together in heavenly places in Christ Jesus (Eph. 2:6).

There is no question as to where Jesus is now. When He had by himself purged our sins, *He "sat down on the right hand of the Majesty on high"* (Heb. 1:3). Therefore, if we sit together in heavenly places in Christ Jesus, and Jesus is now seated at the right hand of God the Father, we KNOW where our life is. *We are seated with Jesus at the right hand of the Majesty.* Positionally, every born again, bloodwashed child of God is just as sure for heaven as if he were already there because in deep spiritual Bible truth, he IS already there!

The instant we are born again, we are baptized into the body of Christ: "For by one Spirit are we all baptized into one body, whether we be Jews or Gentiles, whether we be bond or free; and have been all made to drink into one Spirit" (I Cor. 12:13). We are baptized into the Church of the living God by the Holy Ghost. Christ is the head of the Church, and He is also the foundation.

". . . Christ also loved the Church, and gave Himself for it . . . For we are members of His body, of His flesh, and of His bones" (Eph. 5:25, 30). I see no reason for misunderstanding in answering the question, "Our life — where IS it?"

"Wherefore if ye be dead with Christ from the rudiments of the world, why, as though living in the world, are ye subject to ordinances?" (Col. 2:20). Since believers are dead with Christ, we are not to act as though we were alive in this present evil world. We are partakers with Christ — in his death, burial, and resurrection. Christ died, to die no more. He came into this world, He was crucified, He died IN this world; and insofar as this world is concerned, Christ is a dead man. Thus through His cross we are crucified to the world, and the world is crucified to us.

The Word of God teaches us that God the Father has so completely associated us with the Lord Jesus Christ, His only begotten Son, that He counts us with Him as dead to sin — (study Romans chapter 6). We are also dead to the law — (study Romans chapter 7). We are dead to the world — (study Galatians 6:14). True faith accepts God's record as true, and puts no question mark around His Word, even though we may not fully understand it.

"But YE ARE NOT IN THE FLESH, BUT IN THE SPIRIT, IF SO BE THE SPIRIT OF GOD DWELL IN YOU. NOW IF ANY MAN HAVE NOT THE SPIRIT OF CHRIST, HE IS NONE OF HIS" (Rom. 8:9). Therefore, the life which we possess as believers is not actually *here* — it cannot be, for we are dead; but the life we received from Jesus, the eternal life He gives when we exercise faith in His finished work, is hidden with Christ in God.

What a blessed truth! How wonderful it would be if all believers would accept the record of God and not put question marks around "Thus saith the Lord!" How much it would mean to us as individual believers if we could only realize fully that when we receive Jesus, we are receiving the gift of God — *life eternal*; and this life is IN Jesus. If we would only believe this fact and stand upon it, what power we would possess in giving testimony to the saving and keeping grace of God! What power it would give us over the world, the flesh, the devil.

Since we are dead to the world and risen with Christ, we are to seek those things which are above where Christ sits at the right hand of God. We are to have our minds on things above, not on things here below (Col. 3:1, 2). This means that believers should dwell upon, be occupied with and delight in the place of which we are citizens — yes, citizens NOW.

Thus the tremendous importance of knowing our place and position as born again children of God. We are dead to this world, we are risen with Christ, we are citizens of another world.

WHAT IS OUR DUTY AS WE TRAVEL THIS PILGRIM JOURNEY?

"I am crucified with Christ: nevertheless I live; yet not I, but Christ liveth in me . . ." (Gal. 2:20). Since Christ is our life, since we possess divine nature, since we are the tabernacle of the Holy Ghost, since we have our sufficiency in Jesus and are complete in Him, it is our duty to reveal Christ to all and sundry as we pass through this dark world on our journey toward the Pearly White City.

We are living epistles read of men. Jesus came from heaven's glory, from the Father's bosom, to declare God to man. He declared the love of God in all that He said, in all that He did, in every miracle He performed. And since we are commanded to take up the cross and follow Him, walking in His steps, it is our solemn duty (as well as our glorious privilege) to present Christ to all, through the things we do, the words we speak, the songs we sing, the places we go and the company we keep. We are dead to this world, and we are ALIVE UNTO GOD.

Notice: "Ye are dead. . ." (Col. 3:3).

"Likewise reckon ye also yourselves to be dead indeed unto sin, but alive unto God through Jesus Christ our Lord" (Rom. 6:11).

"Always bearing about in the body the dying of the Lord Jesus, that the life also of Jesus might be made manifest in our body" (II Cor. 4:10).

God in His marvelous saving grace has now taken up His abode in these bodies in the Person of the Holy Spirit, in order that these bodies may become the medium through which Jesus Christ is put on display in a dark and sinful world. It is therefore our solemn responsibility as a child of God, possessing life eternal, to display Christ in all that we are and in all that we do. We should at all times express Christ in every detail of life, *since "He IS our life."*

If we discharge our duties and responsibilities to Christ, this involves the bearing about in our bodies the dying of Jesus. It involves the constant application of the cross. We are to take up the cross *daily*. The cross is the symbol of the power of death — death to all and everything that we were as sons of Adam, the natural man. We are to constantly live in the shadow of the cross, applying the cross in order that nothing pertaining to self will in any way be seen on display in our daily walk. *ONLY that which is of Christ* must be exhibited before the world in all that we say, all that we do, and all that we are.

The spiritually minded believer knows and understands that we cannot allow the flesh to have its way. The Apostle Paul declared, "For I know that in me (that is, in my flesh,) dwelleth no good thing" (Rom. 7:18). If we allow the flesh to have charge of our daily living, we will utterly fail in our stewardship. Salvation is God's gift. Redemption is God's miracle. But cross-bearing and living the life of a good steward and a good soldier is our responsibility since Christ is our life and our bodies are the tabernacles in which He dwells.

As believers who should be displaying Christ in our daily lives, if we are selfish, irritable, and lose our tempers we fail the Lord. Jesus was never selfish. He loved His enemies, and in prayer He said to the Heavenly Father, "Father, forgive them, for they know not what they do." The reproaches of them who reproach us fall on Jesus. He is willing to bear our burdens and carry our sorrows.

Most of us need to stand still and let the Holy Spirit search our hearts. We need to face the solemn fact that in our daily living many times we display far more of our natural characteristics than we do the characteristics of the Lord Jesus Christ. If we live a spiritual life, if we fully discharge our responsibility to Christ, such a life will require contant watchfulness and unwavering fidelity. We cannot let up for one moment. If we give the devil an inch he will take a yard. If we give him a foot he will take a mile. That is the reason Paul said, *"ALWAYS bearing about in the body the dying of the Lord Jesus."* If we relax, if we take a vacation from spiritual things in thought or intent of heart for only a moment, we are in grave danger. The devil takes no vacation; he never relaxes; he is always on the job to trip, to hinder, to rob the believer.

If we are to stand, if we are to be stedfast and unmoveable, we must put on the whole armor of God, that we may do *all that we do* to the glory of God and express Christ in all that we do, for HE IS OUR LIFE. The world judges Christ by the way we live and the things we do.

We must show no mercy in self-judgment. Nothing can be spared. All that we are must be kept under the cross, in the place of death. We dare not allow anything pertaining to the flesh to be resurrected. If we do, we are in grave danger of backsliding and losing our reward at the end of this pilgrim journey.

From whence do we obtain the power to discharge this great responsibility as believers? Such power is found only in Christ. It is found only in being occupied with Christ in glory, seeking those things which are above, looking unto Jesus, the author and finisher of our faith.

"But we all, with open face beholding as in a glass the glory of the Lord, are changed into the same image from glory to glory, even as by the Spirit of the Lord" (II Cor. 3:18). As we seek those things which are above, as we are occupied with the Lord of glory who is seated at the right hand of the Majesty on high, we are continuously transformed; and as we grow in grace and in the knowledge of our Lord and Saviour, Jesus Christ, the likeness of Christ beams forth and we express HIM in our daily routine of life. As we look to the Lord of glory we *reflect* that glory to which we look moment by moment.

Dearly beloved fellow believer, we are not to regard as a figure of speech the statement, "We are crucified with Christ." (The Greek here reads, "We *have been* crucified.") It is not just a figure of speech that we are dead with Christ, that we put off the old man and put on the new. *IN CHRIST we are new creations.* Old things ARE passed away. All things ARE become new. These things are divine realities in God through Christ.

Born again men and women, new creations in Christ Jesus and therefore possessors of divine nature, are distinctly and definitely different from the natural man — sons of Adam who are not regenerated by the power of God. All that we were by Adam's nature, men in the flesh, is gone by way of the cross. We are crucified with Christ, we HAVE BEEN crucified with Christ, we have died to the world. The old man is crucified and only the new man (Christ who is our life) remains. He alone is to be expressed in our walk, in our talk and in everything we do.

Oh, yes — this is a grave responsibilty: but have you stopped to think of the tremendous honor God has conferred upon us as His children? Think of it, beloved! God Almighty — eternal, omniscient, omnipotent, omnipresent, sovereign God — choosing poor, hell-deserving sinners, made new by God's grace through the shed blood of Jesus! And then, as new creatures IN Christ Jesus, God puts His Christ on display in this world, *in US*. Think of it! Our bodies, the tabernacle of the Holy Ghost, the house of divine nature. We — vehicles used of God for the presentation of His Christ in a dark world. Responsibility? Yes! But honor beyond man's imagination — to think that God would allow us so great privilege!

BELIEVERS DISPLAY CHRIST NOW — IN THE FUTURE,

BELIEVERS WILL BE DISPLAYED WITH CHRIST

"For ye are dead, and your life is hid with Christ in God. When Christ, who is our life, shall appear, then shall ye also appear with Him in glory" (Col. 3:3, 4).

The words "who is" are not in the original Greek. The verse reads, "When CHRIST OUR LIFE shall appear. . ." As previously stated, we are now, positionally, seated with Christ in God in the heavenlies — and this is pure Gospel truth. However, we will not be *displayed* with Christ in the heavenlies *in a visible way for all creatures to see*, until the Rapture and the first resurrection.

The dead are resting from their labors now: "Blessed are the dead which die in the Lord from henceforth: Yea, saith the Spirit, that they may rest from their labours; and their works do follow them" (Rev. 14:13). To be absent from this body is to be present with the Lord (II Cor. 5:1-8). When a believer departs this life, he departs this body. The body goes back to dust, but the spirit goes back to God who gave it (Ecc. 12:7).

Paul said, "For me to live is Christ, and to die is gain . . . For I am in a strait betwixt two, having a desire to depart, and to be with Christ; which is far better: Nevertheless to abide in the flesh is more needful for you" (Phil. 1:21-24). When a believer departs this life, the body returns to dust and will remain there until the first resurrection.

In I Thessalonians 4:13-18 we have a clear, understandable outline of the next glorious event for believers and the Church of the living God. The Lord Jesus will descend from heaven with a shout and with the trump of God. The dead in Christ will rise first, and then we who are alive will be changed — *in a moment*; and together we will all be caught up in the clouds to meet the Lord in the air.

". . . When this corruptible shall have put on incorruption, and this mortal shall have put on immortality, then shall be brought to pass the saying that is written, Death is swallowed up in victory" (I Cor. 15:54). Then it is that we shall SEE Him, *and be like Him!* (I John 3:1-3).

The Lord Jesus reserved the right to make this announcement Himself, and He was the first to proclaim: "*I am the resurrection, and the life: he that believeth in me, though he were dead, yet shall he live: and whosoever liveth and believeth in me shall never die*" (John 11:25, 26). These glorious words were spoken to Martha, the brokenhearted sister of Lazarus. In this declaration Jesus positively differentiates between two classes of saints — those who have died (referring to the body), and those who will be living at His return. The saints who have died will be raised first; then those who are alive will be changed: ". . . We shall not all sleep (die), but *we shall all be changed, in a moment, in the twinkling of an eye. . ."* (I Cor. 15:51).

CONVERSION — CONSECRATION — CONSUMMATION

When we receive Jesus Christ as Saviour, we are converted from a life of sin to a new life, because Christ IS our life and when we are truly converted we receive Him by faith and He comes into our hearts in the person of the Holy Spirit. Therefore we become partakers of divine nature.

Bible conversion brings life eternal. We have life when we have Christ. When we receive Christ He *gives* us life. Since our life is Christ (and apart from Him there IS no life); since we are His purchased possession bought with a price; and since it is Bible truth that our body is the tabernacle of the Holy Spirit, then it is our sacred duty (as well as a grand and glorious privilege) to give our life *back* to Jesus in service and allow Him to become LORD of that life.

Paul describes such consecration in these words: "I beseech you therefore, brethren, by the mercies of God, that ye present your bodies a living sacrifice, holy, acceptable unto God, which is your reasonable service. And be not conformed to this world: but be ye transformed by the renewing of your mind, that ye may prove what is that good, and acceptable, and perfect, will of God" (Rom. 12:1, 2).

In Romans 6:13 Paul admonishes us, "Neither yield ye your members as instruments of unrighteousness unto sin: *but yield yourselves unto God, as those that are alive from the dead, and your members as instruments of righteousness unto God."* Those of us who are converted and have life eternal (because Christ is our life) should in return give our lives back to Him in total consecration, and live day by day looking for that blessed consummation — *the return of our Lord Jesus Christ.*

"For the grace of God that bringeth salvation hath appeared to all men, teaching us that, denying ungodliness and worldly lusts, we should live soberly, righteously, and godly, in this present world; looking for that blessed hope, and glorious appearing of the great God and our Saviour Jesus Christ" (Titus 2:11-13).

In these verses we have:

1. *Grace that brings salvation.* That is the beginning.

2. *Godliness.* After grace becomes ours by faith, then grace sets up a classroom in our soul and teaches us to live godly.

3. *Glory* — the consummation of the gift of grace, and its ultimate reward.

Grace brings salvation, grace teaches us to deny ungodliness and practice godliness. And grace teaches us to look for *"that blessed hope"* — which of course is the glorious appearing of the great God and our Saviour, Jesus Christ.

Justification and adoption have to do with true conversion which brings life eternal. Then, after we are converted, identification and Bible sanctification are associated with full consecration to God, permitting Jesus to be the Lord of our lives and we His bondslaves. And *one glorious day* we will be caught up to meet our Lord, and will be glorified with Him. Thus we will experience the consummation of the glorious salvation that begins with conversion, continues in consecration, and ends in the glorious fact that we will have a body just like His resurrection body.

There is no excuse for gloom in the life of a true believer. We have the sure promise that Jesus will receive us unto Himself, and we will be like Him. Just before His crucifixion He told His disciples that He would go into Jerusalem, that He would be arrested, tried, condemned and crucified. This heartbreaking announcement saddened them; and Jesus encouraged them by saying, "Let not your heart be troubled: Ye believe in God, believe also in me. In my Father's house are many mansions: If it were not so, I would have told you. I go to prepare a place for you. And if I go and prepare a place for you,

> I WILL COME AGAIN. . .
> AND RECEIVE YOU UNTO MYSELF. . .
> THAT WHERE I AM, THERE YE MAY BE ALSO"
> (John 14:1-3).

Therefore, do not be troubled. "Rejoice, and be exceeding glad."

This is the promise of Jesus — and His promises do not need an "Amen" from anyone; but notice the words of Paul:

". . . I would not have you to be ignorant, brethren, concerning them which are asleep, that ye sorrow not, even as others which have no hope. For if we believe that Jesus died and rose again, even so them also which sleep in Jesus will God bring with Him. For this we say unto you by the Word of the Lord, that we which are alive and remain unto the coming of the Lord shall not prevent (or precede) them which are asleep.

"FOR THE LORD HIMSELF SHALL DESCEND FROM HEAVEN WITH A SHOUT . . . WE SHALL BE CAUGHT UP . . . TO MEET THE LORD IN THE AIR: AND SO SHALL WE EVER BE WITH THE LORD. Wherefore COMFORT ONE ANOTHER WITH THESE WORDS!!!" (I Thess. 4:13-18).

Regardless of what men say or teach, the Lord Jesus Christ is coming back to this earth personally. He is coming back to make up His jewels. The born again who have departed this life will be raised incorruptible, the living saints will be changed (this mortal will put on immortality) and then together we will be caught up in the clouds to meet the Lord in the air — *and so shall we ever be with our Lord!* These words are indeed comforting to those of us who are believers, possessors of life eternal.

There is a promise of special reward to all who love the appearing of the Lord Jesus: "Henceforth there is laid up for me a crown of righteousness, which the Lord, the righteous Judge, shall give me at that day: and not to me only, but *UNTO ALL THEM THAT LOVE HIS APPEARING*" (II Tim. 4:8).

It was this blessed hope, this fact which is divinely assured in the Word of God, that lifted the Apostle Paul above the circumstances he faced and the horrible persecution that was heaped upon him. He always kept his eyes turned upward, looking for "that blessed hope." But while looking, he was busy witnessing — even when handcuffed to a Roman guard. He never allowed any opportunity for service or witnessing to slip away from him; he bought up every available opportunity to tell others about his wonderful Saviour and *soon coming Christ*.

"For which cause we faint not; but though our outward man perish, yet the inward man is renewed day by day . . . For we know that if our earthly house of this tabernacle were dissolved, we have a building of God, an house not made with hands, eternal in the heavens. For in this we groan, earnestly desiring to be clothed upon with our house which is from heaven: If so be that being clothed we shall not be found naked. For we that are in this tabernacle do groan, being burdened: not for that we would be unclothed, but clothed upon, that mortality might be swallowed up of life" (II Cor. 4:16; 5:1-4).

The life we have is in Christ. *In Christ glorified*, the believer sees power capable of swallowing up and annihilating each and every trace of mortality. We are divinely assured of the fact that Christ was on high in glory before He came into the world, and He is now seated at the right hand of God the Father because He conquered the world, the flesh, and the devil! And because He had the power to conquer, and the power to lay His life down and take it again, He is now seated at the right hand of the Majesty. Because HE lives, we live also. The power that raised up Jesus from the dead will also raise us up and the Spirit will quicken these mortal bodies. Paul did not desire to be unclothed, but clothed, that that which was mortal in him should be absorbed by life. He desired that the mortality that characterized his human nature received from Adam should disappear before the power of life which Paul saw in Jesus Christ — Saviour, Mediator, and coming King.

The life of Jesus was Paul's life, and he knew that even though we die in the flesh, we continue to live in Christ. Jesus said, "That which is born of flesh is flesh; and that which is born of the Spirit is spirit" (John 3:6). The flesh goes back to dust, and the spirit returns to God. In Christ is life — not simply *life,* but *life eternal.*

When Jesus comes in the Rapture and the first resurrection, He will "change our vile body, that it may be fashioned like unto His glorious body, according to the working whereby He is able even to subdue all things unto Himself" (Phil. 3:21).

THEREFORE

The full, complete results of Christ's being our life will not be reached until the Rapture and the first resurrection. We rejoice in the knowledge that we now possess eternal life. We do not look to the resurrection to know that we are saved. We do not look to the resurrection as the time when we come into possession of eternal life — we have eternal life NOW. And since we know that life eternal is in Christ and that He who died for our sins will die no more, we know that our eternal life is unending — *forever.* But we shall one day lose all trace of this mortal body of corruption. We know that life and incorruptibility both have been brought to light in the Gospel, and we who possess Christ will one day possess a body that is incorruptible, immortal (II Tim. 1:10).

I do not profess to fully understand the fact that believers are NOW in Christ, hidden with Christ in God, seated at the right hand of God in Christ, seated in the heavenlies in Christ, dead to the world and alive unto God. I confess readily that in this body of humiliation and through this finite mind I cannot fully appreciate these things. They are *divinely true*, yet we finite creatures can but feebly enter into them now. But we are permitted to look to the heavenlies where Christ is, and seek those things which are above. We see Him there because we know He IS there. Stephen saw Jesus standing at the right hand of God the Father, and testified to that fact (Acts 7:55). We know that Jesus is glorified at the right hand of God the Father. We know He died once, to die no more — death hath no more dominion over Him. And the fact that He died and rose again and is now seated at the right hand of God the Father is our guarantee that the Word of God is true.

And since we have the divine guarantee that the Word of God is true, we have the divine guarantee that He who came the first time to pay the penalty for sin and save our souls will come the second time to redeem the body. We have the divine guarantee that we will be like Him. And then we shall enjoy all the fulness of life — yes, the life which is in Him, the life which He IS. It is a divine Bible fact that every born again, bloodwashed, redeemed child of God is predestined to be conformed to the image of His dear Son, that we might be the firstborn among many brethren (Rom. 8:29).

All this is ours by God's grace — and since it IS all by His grace, to God alone should we give all praise, thanksgiving, and worship.

IN CLOSING

Oh, the glory of it all! We who were dead in trespasses and sins "hath He quickened." We who were dead in trespasses and sins, He raised from the dead and made alive, through His own power. When we were dead in trespasses and sins, we walked according to this dark, ungodly world, and we walked according to the course of the prince of the power of the air — none other than the devil himself. We followed the spirit that worketh in the children of disobedience — the children of Satan. Among these children of Satan we also had our conversation in times past, talking of lust and evil, fulfilling the desires of the flesh and of the mind. We were by nature — the nature in which we were born — children of the devil, even as all are, until born again.

But in spite of our deadness, in spite of our wretchedness, in spite of our ungodliness, in spite of our being without strength and enemies of God, we read, "BUT GOD, who is rich in mercy, for His great love wherewith He loved us, even when we were dead in sins, hath quickened us together with Christ, (by grace ye are saved;) AND HATH RAISED US UP TOGETHER, AND MADE US SIT TOGETHER IN HEAVENLY PLACES IN CHRIST JESUS" (Eph. 2:4-6).

Why did God do this for hell-deserving, wretched children of wrath? "THAT IN THE AGES TO COME HE MIGHT SHEW THE EXCEEDING RICHES OF HIS GRACE IN HIS KINDNESS TOWARD US THROUGH CHRIST JESUS" (Eph. 2:7).

NOW we see why the grace of God was extended to us. We see WHY God allowed Jesus to come into the world, take the sinner's place, bear the sins of the sinner in His own body and nail them to His cross. We understand WHY God saves poor, dead, wretched sinners. In the glorious eternity ahead of us God will put on display in the heavenlies in the Pearly White City, the Church that He purchased with His own blood

— the Church of which every believer is a member — the Church of the living God. We become members of that Church through the Spirit of God in the new birth. When we are born again we are baptized into the body of Christ by the Holy Spirit, and we receive life — the life of Christ — because we are IN Christ, and Christ is in us. But God has wrought this marvelous miracle of mercy through grace in order that God can display the exceeding riches of His grace in His kindness toward us through Christ Jesus, our Saviour and Lord.

It is wonderful to know that one day we who are born again will be God's pearl of great price, displayed in the heavenlies, and we will be viewed from every corner of God's new heaven, new earth, and all the new creation, because all things will be made new.

Through faithful testimony and consecrated living, believers display Christ in a dark world. Then at the end of this pilgrim journey *God will display us* in the Pearly White City, to show the exceeding riches of His grace.

"Beloved, NOW are we the sons of God, and it doth not yet appear what we shall be: but we know that, when He shall appear, we shall be like him; for we shall see Him as He is" (I John 3:2).

We are now God's children, sons of God; but then, in that glorious day we will be displayed with Christ in the home built for the bride by the bridegroom — the place Jesus spoke of when He said, "I go to *prepare* a place for you." True believers are dead to this world. We reckon ourselves dead indeed unto sin, but we are alive unto God. When we appear with the Lord Jesus Christ in glory, then will be displayed the fact that Christ is our life and that we are one with Him IN eternal life. Then shall we reign in life by One — even the Lord Jesus Christ: "For if by one man's offence death reigned by one; much more they which receive abundance of grace and of the gift of righteousness shall reign in life by one, Jesus Christ" (Rom. 5:17).

These bodies will be changed, but the relationship with Christ which we possess now — that is, life in Him — will never be changed. Christ is our life now, Christ will be our life throughout eternity. The relationship that began the moment we believed unto salvation will continue throughout the eternity of eternities. Christ will be the fountain of life forever, and we will walk forever in the light of His life. There will be no more tears, no more heartache, no more sorrow, no more disappointment, no more corruption, NO MORE DEATH — for former things will have passed away (Rev. 21:4).

We read in I Corinthians 15:26 that the last enemy to be destroyed is death; and when that glorious day comes, *death will have been destroyed,* and for each and every saint there will be constant, perpetual, unhindered, eternal enjoyment of life abundant — the life that is ours, now and forever, through Him who died, rose again, is now alive to die no more.

What a tremendous contrast to our present circumstances in this vale of tears! We live in a world of darkness, and yet we possess light and life — light that can never be dimmed, life that can never be snuffed out, because our life and light are in Christ. We are children of the day, and we look forward to that glorious day when we will be like HIM.

Are YOU saved? Are you born again? If not, get a Bible, read John 5:24, Romans 10:9, 10, Acts 16:31, Ephesians 2:8, 9. Then bow your head and in your own words ask God the Father to save you, by grace through faith in the finished work and the shed blood of Jesus the Son. Just simply ask God to have mercy on you for Christ's sake and save your soul — and He will!

"I am come that they might have life, and that they might have it more abundantly" (John 10:10).

CHRIST OUR LORD

CHRIST OUR LORD

THIS JESUS HATH GOD RAISED UP, WHEREOF WE ALL ARE WIT-
NESSES. Therefore being by the right hand of God exalted,
and having received of the Father the promise of the Holy
Ghost, He hath shed forth this, which ye now see and hear.
For David is not ascended into the heavens: but he saith himself, The Lord said unto my Lord, Sit thou on my right hand,
until I make thy foes thy footstool. Therefore let all the
house of Israel know assuredly, that God hath made that same
Jesus, whom ye have crucified, both *Lord* and *Christ*" (Acts
2:32-36).

In these verses, Peter *declares* Jesus to be both Lord and
Christ. The title "Lord" as given to the Saviour, in its full
significance rests upon the *bodily resurrection* of Jesus.
Thomas, when he realized the significance of the presence of a
mortal wound in the body of a living man, immediately joined
with it the absolute title of Deity, saying, "*My Lord and my
God!*" (John 20:28).

155

The apostle Paul declared the same truth, after first pointing out the self-humbling of Christ:

"Let this mind be in you, which was also in Christ Jesus: Who, being in the form of God, thought it not robbery to be equal with God: But made Himself of no reputation, and took upon Him the form of a servant, and was made in the likeness of men: And being found in fashion as a man, He humbled Himself, and became obedient unto death, even the death of the cross."

Paul then points out the *exaltation* of the Christ who became obedient unto death, even the death of the cross:

"WHEREFORE God also hath highly exalted Him, and given Him a name which is above every name: That at the name of Jesus every knee should bow, of things in heaven, and things in earth, and things under the earth; and that *every tongue should confess that JESUS CHRIST IS LORD, to the glory of God the Father*" (Phil. 2:5-11).

After He had laid down His life for the sins of the world and God had raised Him bodily from the dead, the Lord Jesus Himself said, "*ALL power is given me in heaven and in earth*" (Matt. 28:18).

In II Peter 2:1 we are warned that in the last days there will be false teachers and lying prophets who shall "brings in damnable heresies, even *denying the LORD* that bought them . . ." One of the most damnable heresies of false teachers and ministers of the devil is to deny the Lordship of Jesus!

Christ IS Lord indeed over all the earth, Lord over *all;* but He is Lord of the believer in a much stronger, closer relationship than His lordship over all creation. Since He has saved us from our sins and redeemed us from all iniquity, He has a perfect right to be Lord over our lives in all that we are or ever hope to be, in all that we have or ever hope to have.

God the Father has made Christ the Son to be Lord, on the grounds of His redemptive work. He has given to Christ this place of universal supremacy as a result of the price Jesus paid to redeem — not only man, but in the fulness of redemption — *the whole creation* (Rom. 8:22). There is a day coming when all creation will be delivered from the curse.

If we speak reverently and humbly, with much fear and trembling, we may say that God has exalted Christ to this universal supremacy as Lord of all *in appreciation* of the sacrificial death Jesus died to bring about redemption.

When Jesus was baptized, God the Father said, "This is my beloved Son, in whom I am well pleased" (Matt. 3:17). Again, on the Mount of Transfiguration God the Father said, "This is my beloved Son, in whom I am well pleased; hear ye Him" (Matt. 17:5). In John 12:28 Jesus prayed, "Father, glorify thy name. *Then came there a voice from heaven,* saying, I have both glorified it, and will glorify it again." When the people standing near by heard the voice, some said that it thundered; others said, "An angel spake to Him."

In John 8:29 Jesus said, ". . . He that sent me is with me: The Father hath not left me alone; *for I do always those things that please Him.*" In John 10:17 He said, "Therefore doth my Father love me, because I lay down my life, that I might take it again."

In view of what the Scriptures tell us, I do not feel that it is wrong to say that God the Father has exalted Jesus to the place of universal supremacy as Lord over all in appreciation for the life He lived on earth and the sacrificial death He died in order that poor sinners might be redeemed — and finally, according to God's program, that *all creation might be redeemed* from the curse that came *upon* all creation because of Adam's sin. The first Adam was responsible for bringing the curse upon all creation. *The last Adam* (Jesus) bought back, at the tremendous price of His blood, all that the first Adam lost.

In Matthew 13:44 we read, ". . . The Kingdom of Heaven is like unto treasure hid in a field; the which when a man hath

found, he hideth, and for joy thereof goeth and selleth all
that he hath, and buyeth that field." In reality, Jesus acquired lordship *over all* through the purchase price of His
blood. He emptied Himself. In one gigantic step he came
from the Father's bosom in heaven's glory to earth's sorrows
and willingly laid down His life, and through His shed blood
He purchased all that Adam had surrendered to the enemy.

"These words spake Jesus, and lifted up His eyes to
heaven, and said, Father, the hour is come; glorify thy Son,
that thy Son also may glorify thee: AS THOU HAST GIVEN
HIM POWER' OVER ALL FLESH, THAT HE SHOULD
GIVE ETERNAL LIFE TO AS MANY AS THOU HAST
GIVEN HIM" (John 17:1, 2).

The Greek word translated "power" in this passage signi-
fies having power or authority and could have been properly
rendered *authority*. Thus, through the purchase price paid,
Jesus has been appointed by God to have AUTHORITY over
all flesh.

In Acts 10:36 Peter testifies: "The Word which God sent
unto the children of Israel, preaching peace by Jesus Christ
(HE IS LORD OF ALL.)"

LORDSHIP AS HAVING TO DO
WITH BELIEVERS

As previously stated, Christ's lordship in relation to believers goes deeper than His lordship over all creation. He
is Lord of creation by divine appointment of God the Father
(John 17:2), but His lordship in relation to believers is the
same as that between master and slave. Believers are bond-
servants of Jesus Christ, and when we have presented our
bodies a living sacrifice, our members as instruments of righteousness, and have done all that is commanded us, we still
have nothing about which to boast and brag for we have done

only our duty and our reasonable service. We are the purchased possession of Jesus Christ, OUR LORD.

Yet our relation to Christ as our Lord, in the spiritual sense goes far beyond that of a servant to an earthly master. Believers have, by the grace of God, become children of God; and when we realize the great miracle that has been wrought in our hearts through faith in the shed blood of Jesus Christ, we have been brought to the place where we are not only willing, but *happy,* to own our position as servants — yea, as *bondslaves* — to Jesus Christ. He has a perfect right to be Lord of our lives since we are sons of God *because of HIS tremendous sacrifice* — His death on the cross.

By the grace of God, Jesus tasted death for every man (Heb. 2:9).

Without shedding of blood there is no remission of sins (Heb. 9:22).

It is the precious blood of Jesus (not corruptible things) that redeems us (I Pet. 1:18ff.).

The blood of Jesus Christ, God's Son, cleanses us from all sin (I John 1:7).

We are sons of God — not through any merit on our part, not through anything that we are able to do or give — *but simply because we have received Jesus by faith,* putting our trust in His shed blood which is the price He paid to redeem sinners.

Having trusted in the finished work of Jesus Christ, realizing that sins are forgiven and that we are now sons of God (I John 3:2) we are happy to recognize and accept Christ's authority and His rule in our lives. Realizing what Christ has wrought in our lives, we are happy to take the place of subjection and humbly bow at His feet, confessing that He IS Lord of our lives: "Delight thyself also in the Lord; and He shall give thee the desires of thine heart" (Psalm 37:4).

Jesus died — not only to redeem us and make us sons of God, but "He died for all, *that they which live should not henceforth live unto themselves, BUT UNTO HIM WHICH DIED FOR THEM, AND ROSE AGAIN"* (II Cor. 5:15).

In Romans 14:7-9 we read, "For none of us liveth to himself, and no man dieth to himself. For whether we live, we live unto the Lord; and whether we die, we die unto the Lord: Whether we live therefore, or die, WE ARE THE LORD'S. For to this end Christ both died, and rose and revived, THAT HE MIGHT BE LORD BOTH OF THE DEAD AND LIVING!"

We recognize that Christ is Lord of all, but we must also recognize that He is Lord of the believer in a much more intimate way. He who was in the bosom of the Father humbled Himself for our sakes and became in fashion as a man; and in the body of humiliation He became obedient unto death — even the horrible, indescribable death of the cross. He who is the Christ of God, the Son of God's love, but was rejected and crucified, is now the glorified Man seated at the right hand of God the Father (I Tim. 2:5; Heb. 1:1-3).

He acquired authority over us through His shed blood, and when we realize the tremendous price He paid for our redemption we will with joy confess Him as Lord, giving Him lordship of all that we are and yielding to His authority in all that we do.

Those who refuse to confess God's Christ as Saviour of their souls and Lord of their lives while here upon this earth, who refuse to bend the knee and call upon His holy, saving name, will be *forced* to do so at the great white throne judgment of God: *"That at the name of Jesus every knee should bow, of things in heaven, and things in earth, and things under the earth; and that every tongue should confess that Jesus Christ is LORD, to the glory of God the father"* (Phil. 2:10, 11).

"For it is written, As I live, saith the Lord, every knee shall bow to me, and every tongue shall confess to God" (Rom. 14:10, 11).

Those who on earth refuse to bend the knee to God and confess Jesus as the Christ of God and *Lord of all* will be *forced* to do it in the judgment day — but the verdict then will be altogether different. Those who confess Him as Saviour and then as Lord of their lives on earth will one day hear Him say, "Well done, thou good and faithful servant . . . enter thou into the joy of thy Lord." But those who *refuse* to confess Him here will then be forced to confess Him — and they will hear Him say, "Depart from me, ye that work iniquity. *I never knew you!*"

"And these shall go away into everlasting punishment: but the righteous into life eternal" (Matt. 25:46). My dear friend, if you are so unfortunate as to be one of those dear people who refuse to bow before Almighty God and confess His Son Jesus while here upon this earth — *remember*: If you refuse to do it willingly here, God will *force* you to do it at the judgment; for there, *every* knee shall bow and *every* tongue will confess that Jesus Christ is LORD.

It is the divine duty of every believer to recognize Jesus as Lord of his life, to declare Him as such and to be subject to His divine authority *in every detail* of life. In so doing, we who name His name can in some small measure witness for Him in this day when He is rejected of men and pushed aside by the masses.

THE BELIEVER'S RESPONSIBILITY TO CHRIST AS LORD

It is a divine fact that *God so loved us* that He gave His only begotten Son that we, through His death, might be saved. It is a divine fact that *Jesus* so loved us that even in His darkest hour, since there was no one else to pay the ransom, He was willing to drink the black and bitter cup — and DID drink it, to the last bitter dregs — that we might be sons of

God through faith in His shed blood. In view of these divine truths, what is our responsibility to HIM as Lord of our lives?

Our paramount responsibility is to love the Lord with all our hearts, with all of our souls, with all of our minds and our strength (Matt. 22:37). We are to love Him first and foremost above everything else. Jesus said to His disciples, "If any man come to me, and hate not his father, and mother, and wife, and children, and brethren, and sisters, yea, and his own life also, he cannot be my disciple. And whosoever doeth not bear the cross, and come after me, cannot be my disciple" (Luke 14:26, 27). Jesus did not mean here that we are to actually hate our loved ones. He simply meant that we are not to allow anyone or anything — even our own dear loved ones or our deepest desires — to come between us and our Lord.

Jesus instructed us, "As the Father hath loved me, so have I loved you: continue ye in my love. If ye keep my commandments, ye shall abide in my love; even as I have kept my Father's commandments, and abide in HIS love. These things have I spoken unto you, that my joy might remain in you, and that your joy might be full. This is my commandment, That ye love one another, as I have loved you. Greater love hath no man than this, that a man lay down his life for his friends. Ye are my friends, if ye do whatsoever I command you" (John 15:9-14).

"We love Him, because He first loved us" (I John 4:19). Since God the Father so loved us that He gave the very best that His power and love could provide; and since God the Son gave *His all* that we might become sons of God, then we should recognize Him as Lord of our lives, and love Him supremely. We should not love anything or anybody above the love we have for Jesus — Saviour, Redeemer, and LORD.

Believers owe the Lord their very best in stewardship. It is not only a grand and glorious *privilege* to serve God and work for Jesus, but it is a great responsibility. We are

bought with a matchless price, we are His purchased posses-
sions and therefore his bondslaves. We owe Him *our very
best* in stewardship.

The last command of Jesus to His disciples was, "Go ye
therefore, and teach all nations, baptizing them in the name
of the Father, and of the Son, and of the Holy Ghost: Teaching them to observe all things whatsoever I have commanded
you: and, lo, I am with you alway, even unto the end of the
world!" (Matt. 28:19, 20).

In John 15:16, 17 He said to them, "Ye have not chosen
me, but I have chosen you, and ordained you, that ye should
go and bring forth fruit, and that your fruit should remain:
that whatsoever ye shall ask of the Father in my name, He
may give it you. These things I command you, that ye love
one another."

Just before Jesus was taken back up into heaven He instructed His disciples to tarry in Jerusalem and wait for the
promise of the Father: "But ye shall receive power, after that
the Holy Ghost is come upon you: and ye shall be witnesses
unto me both in Jerusalem, and in all Judaea, and in Samaria,
and unto the uttermost part of the earth" (Acts 1:8, 9).

We are saved to serve. We glorify God in our disciple-
ship when we bear much fruit (John 15:8). We are saved to
win others. The dearest thing to the great heart of God is
to rescue the soul that is lost in the darkness of sin. In Luke
15:3-7 Jesus pictures this for us: "And He spake this parable
unto them, saying, What man of you, having an hundred
sheep, if he lose one of them, doth not leave the ninety and
nine in the wilderness, and go after that which is lost, until
he find it? And when he hath found it, he layeth it on his
shoulders, rejoicing, and when he cometh home, he calleth
together his friends and neighbours, saying unto them, Rejoice with me; for I have found my sheep which was lost.
I say unto you, that likewise joy shall be in heaven over

one sinner that repenteth, more than over ninety and nine just persons, which need no repentance!"

Later in the same chapter, He gives the parable of the prodigal son, who departed from home of his own free will, taking with him his share of the inheritance, which he wasted in riotous living; and then one day, when the son "came to himself . . . he arose and came to his father. But when he was yet A GREAT WAY OFF, his father saw him, and had compassion, and ran, and fell on his neck, and kissed him. And the son said unto him, Father, I have sinned against heaven, and in thy sight, and am no more worthy to be called thy son. But the father said to his servants, Bring forth the best robe, and put it on him; and put a ring on his hand, and shoes on his feet: And bring hither the fatted calf, and kill it; and let us eat, and be merry: For this my son was dead, and is alive again; he was lost, and is found. And they began to be merry" (Luke 15:11-24 in part).

The father never ceased looking in the direction where the prodigal had disappeared, and the moment he reappeared on the horizon his father did not wait for him to come and apologize, but ran and fell on his neck and kissed him. Jesus is interested in the lost sheep and the prodigals, and He wants those who are His servants to go out in the highways and byways and bring them in.

CHRIST'S COMPASSION

Believers are to get in the yoke with Jesus; we are to take up the cross and follow in His steps. In his epistles Paul often invited his converts to follow HIM as he followed in the footsteps of Jesus.

Since Jesus is our Lord, we should follow Him in love, tenderness, and compassion, looking on the fields that are white unto harvest. Jesus said to His disciples, "Say not ye, There are yet four months, and then cometh harvest. Behold, I say unto you, Lift up your eyes, and look on the fields; for they are white already to harvest" (John 4:35).

In the Gospels we read of how our Lord was moved with compassion: In Matthew 9:36 He saw the scattered multitudes and "was *moved with compassion* on them, because they fainted, and were scattered abroad, as sheep having no shepherd."

In Matthew 14:14 we read, "And Jesus went forth, and saw a multitude, and was *moved with compassion* toward them, and He healed their sick."

In Matthew 15:32 He saw the hungry multitude, and his heart was *moved with compassion.*

In Matthew 20:29-34, as He departed from Jericho He saw two blind men sitting by the wayside, and he *had compassion on them,* touched their eyes, and gave them their sight.

In Mark 1:41 a leper came to Jesus, and, *moved with compassion,* He touched the leper and healed him.

In Luke 7:13, He saw the brokenhearted widow of Nain, and her grief touched His own heart. He *had compassion* on her and restored her son to life.

In Luke 10:30-37 we read of the Good Samaritan (a type of the Lord Jesus Christ). A poor man had fallen among thieves, had been robbed, stripped of his clothing, wounded and left half dead. Others passed him by; but the Good Samaritan *had compassion on him,* bound up his wounds, put him on his own beast, took him to an inn and paid the bill to have him cared for.

Jesus is our example. The same Jesus who died to save us, the Christ of God who left the bosom of the Father and in a body of flesh did what the law could not do that through His sacrifice we might become sons of God, should be recognized as LORD of our lives, and we should allow Him to fill OUR lives with compassion.

In this poor, sick, hungry, blind world of prodigals, and

wounded, robbed, half-dead men we should show forth the compassion of our Lord. We should go to the lost, feed them and bind up their wounds. We should turn on the light of the Gospel so that their blinded minds can be opened. We should tell them the remedy for the leprosy of sin. We should search until we find the sheep that is lost. Remember Jesus said, ". . . *There is joy in the presence of the angels of God over one sinner that repenteth!*" (Luke 15:10).

I ask myself, Have I come to the place in my Christian experience where I realize that I am not my own? My time is not my own, my energy is not my own, and my money is only entrusted to me for awhile. Have I realized that I belong to Jesus Christ my Lord, and that I owe Him *first place* in my time, in my endeavors, in whatsoever I am or whatever I possess? Have I put Him *first* in all things — or am I a slothful servant of God — selfish in my desires and practices of life? Do I sow sparingly, rather than bountifully? Have I come to the place where I have surrendered completely to Him who saved me? *Have I allowed Him to become, truly, LORD of my life?*

"The disciple is not above his master, nor the servant above his lord. It is enough for the disciple that he be as his master, and the servant as his lord . . ." (Matt. 10:24, 25).

The faithful servant, the steward who gives his best to his Lord, will hear these words: "Well done, thou good and faithful servant: Thou hast been faithful over a few things, I will make thee ruler over many things: Enter thou into the joy of thy Lord" (Matt. 25:21). But the servant who has been selfish, lazy, and slothful, occupied with "things" instead of seeking first the kingdom of God and giving first place to the work of the kingdom, will see his stewardship burned: "If any man's work shall be burned, he shall suffer loss: but he himself shall be saved; yet so as by fire" (I Cor. 3:15).

In His parable of service in Luke 17:7-10 Jesus said,

*". . . When ye shall have done all those things which are com-
manded you, say, WE ARE UNPROFITABLE SERVANTS:
WE HAVE DONE THAT WHICH WAS OUR DUTY TO
DO."*

GOD'S BEST — GOD'S SECOND BEST

God the Father *wants to give His best* to ALL of His
children — but He can honor us only as we honor His Son.
God blesses us on the merit of the finished work of Jesus, and
our blessings depend upon our degree of consecration and
surrender to Jesus as Lord of our lives. *Redemption is a gift*
— but to be a disciple, a faithful servant and a good steward is
costly in many ways. The Bible tells of some to whom God
could not give His best because of their hesitation and unbelief. They preferred a way other than God's way, and He
was therefore compelled to give them second best.

God called Abraham to go directly to the land of Canaan — but Abraham made a second choice. He stayed at
Haran for awhile (Gen. 11:31), until the Lord spoke to him
again: "Now the Lord *had said* unto Abram, Get thee out of
thy country, and from thy kindred, and from thy father's
house, unto a land that I will shew thee" (Gen. 12:1). Notice
the past tense in this verse: "The Lord HAD SAID. . ." And
in Acts 7:4 we read of Abraham, ". . . *When his father was
dead,* he removed him into this land. . ." This statement plainly points out that *death* had to snap the bond between parent
and son — the tie that caused Abraham to tarry in Haran
when God had clearly directed him to go to Canaan.

Abraham was a great man. He was called "the friend
of God" (James 2:23); but he took *second best* when he could
have had God's *very* best.

Lot, the nephew of Abraham, was only a second-rate
believer. It is not by accident that the Holy Spirit records,
"So Abram departed, as the Lord had spoken unto him; AND

LOT WENT WITH HIM" (Gen. 12:4). Lot started wrong. *Abraham* went with God, even though it was God's second call to which he responded; but we are not told that LOT went with God. *Lot went with Abraham,* his uncle.

Notice also that "Lot lifted up his eyes, and beheld all the plain of Jordan, that it was well watered every where . . . Then *Lot chose him* all the plain of Jordan . . ." (Gen. 13:10, 11 in part). But Abraham did not look upon the land *until God told him to look*: "And the Lord said unto Abram, after that Lot was separated from him, Lift up now thine eyes, and look from the place where thou art northward, and southward, and eastward, and westward: *For all the land which thou seest, to thee will I give it,* and to thy seed for ever" (Gen. 13:14, 15).

Even though Peter clearly tells us that Lot was a just man (II Pet. 2:7) — and there is no doubt in my mind that Lot is in Paradise today — his look at Sodom certainly cost him dearly! (And if we, as believers, look in the wrong direction instead of looking to the Lord to direct us, it will cost US, too.)

God called Moses to deliver a message to Pharoah and to the children of Israel (Ex. 3:1-14); but Moses hesitated. He explained to God that he was "slow of speech, and of a slow tongue" (Ex. 4:10). In other words, he excused himself because of a speech impediment, and God had to appoint Aaron to be the spokesman. If you will study the Scripture you will find that *Aaron* received the number-one blessing while Moses got second best!

The same truth is set forth again in Numbers 11:11-17. Moses complained. He said unto the Lord, "Wherefore hast thou afflicted thy servant? And wherefore have I not found favour in thy sight, *that thou layest the burden of all this people upon ME?*" Thus, instead of resting upon Moses alone, the Spirit was distributed among the seventy elders for administrative purposes. Moses could have been the ONE through whom the Spirit ministered, but instead, there were *seventy* appointed to this ministry.

The *children of Israel* made a second choice. God had been so real to them, He had blessed and cared for them as for no other people who ever lived upon this earth — but they made their own choice and received God's second best. *They chose to wander in the wilderness instead of entering the promised land immediately.* Oh, yes — it is true that they had many great experiences with the Lord and witnessed many miracles; but they would have had far greater blessing had they entered into His rest (Heb. 3:8-11).

Martha made a second choice. She was excited, anxious, and cumbered with "many things." Jesus was the dinner guest in that home, and she chose to show Him the very best in service; but Mary sat at His feet and fed from His wonderful words of life. Mary chose the best, Martha the second best (Luke 10:38-42).

Peter, James, and John chose second best. They were honored by being invited to go with Jesus to the Mount of Transfiguration, but *they slept* while Jesus met with Moses and Elijah. They discussed His coming death on the cross to pay the sin-debt and purchase redemption for all who will trust in His finished work, but the three disciples missed that glorious event.

After the conversation had ended, just before Moses and Elijah departed, *they awakened* — and Peter shouted, "It is good for us to be here!"

He then wanted to build three tabernacles there, and remain on the mountain top. Had Peter chosen *the best,* and heard the discussion that had just taken place, he would not have *wanted* to remain on the mountain top. He would have been ready to follow as Jesus led the disciples back down the mountainside to the valley filled with needy souls! It is glorious indeed to be with Jesus on the mountain top —

but the place where we can bring more glory to HIM is in the valley of dying souls (Luke 9:28-36; Matt. 17:1-8).

The Lord is looking for believers who have warm hearts filled with compassion that only *He* can place in the heart. He is searching for willing hands — hands that will do His bidding. He is looking for wise heads that will look to Him for direction and leadership. When the believer with a *wise head* is willing to allow the Lord to direct his life, when hands, head, feet, and heart are influenced by the warmth of compassion and love, that believer will be among God's great saints and will bring honor to God the Father through faithful service to Jesus, Lord of his life.

Since He IS our Lord, we should *"abound to every good work"* (II Cor. 9:8).

We should be *"fruitful* in every good work" (Col. 1:10).

We should allow Him to *"stablish (us)* in every good word and work" (II Thess. 2:17).

We should diligently *"follow* every good work" (I Tim. 5:10).

We should allow HIM to make us *"prepared* unto every good work" (II Tim. 2:21).

We should be *"ready* to every good work" (Tit. 3:1).

We should look unto Jesus who is able to make us *"perfect* in every good work" (Heb. 31:21).

And at all times we should remember that *"we are HIS workmanship, CREATED IN CHRIST JESUS UNTO GOOD WORKS, which God hath before ordained that we should walk in them"* (Eph. 2:10).

God has never saved a sinner to sit idle while others serve. His name shall be called JESUS, Saviour — but He is also God's Christ, and HE SHOULD be Lord of everyone whom He has saved.

WE SHOULD WORSHIP HIM AS LORD

In Psalm 45:11 we read, ". . . He is thy Lord . . . worship thou Him." Earlier in the message I pointed out that every knee *should* bow to Jesus here on earth, and those who refuse to bow here will be *forced* to bow at the great White Throne judgment, only to hear Him say, "Depart, I never knew you." However, believers should not only bow before Him as Lord: We should also bow upon our knees before Him in worship, confessing "that Jesus Christ is Lord, to the glory of God the Father" (Phil. 2:11).

In the deep sense of things spiritual, we know that God the Father and God the Son are co-equal and that Jesus should be worshipped as God just as surely and truly as we worship *God the Father* as God; but we must also recognize that it was the same Jesus whom the Jews crucified and buried that God brought back from the grave and made both Lord and Christ. It was that same Jesus who was taken up as MAN and whom God exalted to the right hand of the Majesty on high. He ascended to receive again the glory which He had with the Father before the world was (Heb. 12:2).

It is a great mistake to recognize Jesus Christ as *Man* on earth, as *Man* on the cross — and then forget that He is also Man in *heaven.* "For there is one God, and one Mediator between God and men, the MAN Christ Jesus" (I Tim. 2:5). He was both God and man as He tabernacled here on earth; and He is man (yet co-equal with God) as He sits at the right of the Majesty on high (Heb. 1:1-3).

The scriptural truth of the matter is that when Jesus was on earth He was truly man, the same as He was truly God, and *He was here to declare God TO man* — which He did. But He lost none of His divinity, either here on earth, in the tomb, or NOW as He sits at the right hand of God, as man. He is there to mediate between us and a holy God.

Jesus lived here as WE live, He was tempted in all points

as we are tempted, yet without sin; He became weary, hungry, thirsty, disappointed. He wept, He rejoiced. *Knowing that He lived here on earth as a MAN* and that He is NOW man, seated at the right hand of God, we should be happy to surrender to Him as Lord of our lives. We should be overjoyed for the privilege — not only of turning soul and spirit over to Him for redemption, but of allowing Him to be Lord of our lives in every detail.

It is true that we should worship Him as GOD. We should direct to Him all the adoration that we direct to *God the Father*. When we speak of God, we are speaking of *ONE God manifest in three Persons*. But the Lord of our lives is the Man who is in glory, who sits at the right hand of the Majesty on high — the Man Christ Jesus, who was tempted in all points as we are, yet without sin. He IS Jesus Christ our Lord, who was touched with the feeling of our infirmities, and we should bow before Him to praise Him and to worship Him as Lord of our lives. We should thank GOD for loving us so much that He gave Jesus to save us. It is perfectly in order to name the name of Jesus and thank HIM for saving us. But we should not forget to also *worship* Him as Lord of our lives.

On three occasions, God spoke in an audible voice concerning Jesus while He was here on earth, before He went to Calvary to pay sin's debt. If God was so highly pleased with His Son here on earth, *since* Calvary God undoubtedly esteems Him much greater, and has exalted Him to a much higher position, even at His own right hand. He has given to the Son the highest place in heaven, where He is the object of the love, adoration, and worship of not only the saints, but also of angels and cherubim.

John the Beloved writes, "And they sung a new song, saying, *THOU ART WORTHY* to take the book, and to open the seals thereof: for thou wast slain, and hast redeemed us to God by thy blood out of every kindred, and tongue, and people, and nation; and hast made us unto our God kings and priests: and we shall reign on the earth. And I beheld, and I heard the voice of many angels round about the throne and the beasts and the elders: and the number of them was ten thousand times ten thousand, and thousands of thousands; Saying with a loud voice, WORTHY IS THE LAMB THAT WAS SLAIN TO RECEIVE POWER, AND RICHES, AND WISDOM, AND STRENGTH, AND HONOUR, AND GLORY, AND BLESSING.

"And every creature which is in heaven, and on the earth, and under the earth, and such as are in the sea, and all that are in them, heard I saying, BLESSING, AND HONOUR, AND GLORY, AND POWER, BE UNTO HIM THAT SITTETH UPON THE THRONE, AND UNTO THE LAMB FOR EVER AND EVER. And the four beasts said, Amen. And the four and twenty elders fell down and worshipped Him that liveth for ever and ever" (Rev. 5:9-14).

Since we are bought with the price of His blood, it should be our joy to yield to Him as LORD, and praise and worship Him as Lord of our lives.

BELIEVERS SHOULD PRAY TO HIM AS LORD

Seven centuries before Jesus was born, Isaiah wrote by divine revelation: "For unto us a child is born, unto us a son is given: and the government shall be upon His shoulder: and His name shall be called Wonderful, Counsellor, The mighty God, The everlasting Father, The Prince of Peace" (Isa. 9:6).

We read in the New Testament that His name shall be called JESUS, Saviour. Then we read of CHRIST, His heavenly name. We read of JESUS CHRIST, and of CHRIST JESUS. We read of THE LORD JESUS CHRIST. These different arrangements of His name are not by accident.

We look to Jesus for salvation. He was born JESUS,

to save sinners — and He saves us one time only. *When we are saved, we are ETERNALLY saved.* We become partakers of the divine nature of God, possessors of the Holy Spirit, and our names are written in heaven.

We are saved by His grace; but as believers we are pilgrims in a strange land; and as long as we remain in this tabernacle of flesh, needs will arise. Jesus invites us, "Ask, and it shall be given you; seek, and ye shall find; knock, and it shall be opened unto you" (Matt. 7:7). James 4:3 tells us, "Ye ask, and receive not, because ye ask amiss. . ."

Several prayers prayed by believers are recorded in the New Testament. In Acts 7:54-60 we read of the stoning of Stephen as he called upon God, saying, "LORD JESUS, receive my spirit." Stephen was saved by grace through faith in the finished work of Jesus the Saviour, and if ever man surrendered to Jesus as Lord of his life, surely Stephen did. Therefore, when he was dying, he looked toward heaven and prayed to his LORD, seated at the right hand of God the Father. *Jesus* had already saved his soul, and now he looked to his LORD to receive his spirit.

Paul prayed concerning the thorn in his flesh: "For this thing I besought the LORD thrice, that it might depart from me. And He said unto me, My grace is sufficient for thee: for my strength is made perfect in weakness" (II Cor. 12:8, 9). On the Damascus road, blinded by a light from heaven, Paul fell to the earth, and he heard a voice speaking to him. He asked, "Who art thou, LORD?" The answer was, "I am *Jesus*."

Being a Jew and a Pharisee, Paul spoke in the terms of Jehovah; but he could not know Christ as "LORD" until he had first trusted JESUS as Saviour. Then after he was saved, he prayed to the LORD concerning the thorn in his flesh.

The LORD is responsible for the needs of His servants. We look to JESUS to save us; then Jesus our Saviour has every right to become Jesus our LORD — exercising complete con-

trol in all that we do. He now sits at God's right hand as
Christ Jesus our Mediator, thus we are "complete in HIM"
(Col. 2:10). He is able to sustain us and supply our every
need — be the need spiritual or physical.

But we are also looking for "the glorious appearing of the
great God and our Saviour Jesus Christ." It is Christ the
King who will return in glory to receive us unto Himself.

When the women came to the sepulchre on the resurrection morn, bringing spices and sweet odours to the tomb,
they discovered that the stone had been rolled away from
the door and the body of Jesus was not there. The angel
said to them, "Fear not ye: for I know that *ye seek Jesus,
which was crucified.* He is not here: for He is risen, as He
said. Come, *see the place where the LORD lay*" (Matt.
28:5, 6). Thus did the angel remind the women that *Jesus*
whom they sought — *the man Jesus* with whom they had
walked, talked, and fellowshipped, was now LORD. God
the Father had raised Him — had "promoted" Him, so to
speak; and He is now both Christ AND Lord.

Jesus is the Saviour of sinners. He came as Jesus — not
to be ministered unto, but to minister and to give His life a
ransom for many. But this same Jesus who laid His life down
is LORD OF THE HARVEST, and He instructed His disciples, "Pray ye therefore the LORD of the harvest, that He will
send forth labourers into His harvest" (Matt. 9:38).

The fact that Jesus is Lord of the believer not only constitutes a definite and rightful claim upon us, but also gives
us divine assurance. He has a claim on us because of the
relationship into which we have passed through His finished
work on Calvary. We have been taken out of the kingdom of
darkness and placed into the kingdom of light. We are
removed from the kingdom of Satan and placed into the
family of God. We are assured of this because His Word declares, ". . . He that heareth my Word, and believeth on Him
that sent me, hath everlasting life, and shall not come into

condemnation: but is passed from death unto life" (John 5:24). Please notice here that Jesus used *present tense* — ". . . IS passed from death unto life."

Believers have assurance — not only that condemnation is gone and we are NOW sons of God — but also, since Christ is our LORD and we are His servants, *He will take care of our every need*. Since He IS our Lord, it is a sin for us to do less than trust Him in everything, believe Him for our every need, and desire only that which will bring glory to His name and be of benefit to mankind. Along with the disciples of old, we need to ask, "*LORD, teach us to pray!*"

It is no accident that Paul referred to himself as a servant (Rom. 1:1; Phil. 1:1). The Greek term means a slave or bondslave, and the people to whom Paul ministered understood well the relationship between a slave (or servant) and master. The servant looked to his master IN everything, FOR everything, and the master was responsible for every need of his servant.

As servants of the Lord, our will should be completely lost in HIS will. We should pray as HE prayed: "*Thy* will, *not mine,* be done." We should never be anxious about the things He is able to do for us — and WILL do for us if we will only let Him. If we seek Him first, He will add all else needed — all things that will glorify Him.

Paul said, "I am crucified with Christ: nevertheless I live; yet not I, but Christ liveth in me: and the life which I now live in the flesh I live by the faith of the Son of God, who loved me, and gave Himself for me" (Gal. 2:20). Paul is really saying here, "Christ was crucified for me, I have accepted His crucifixion, and therefore I have received all the benefits of His death. I am alive — and yet it is not I, but *Christ living in me.*"

Our responsibility as servants to our Lord is *obedience.* Jesus said, "Why call ye me, Lord, Lord, and do not the things which I say?" (Luke 6:46). Our bodies should be surrendered to Him as organs for the expression of Himself. We should have no will of our own — we should be completely subject to HIS will. To His disciples He said, "Ye call me Master and LORD: and ye say well; for SO I AM" (John 13:13).

We should live every moment of every day in the attitude of, "LORD, WHAT WILT THOU HAVE ME TO DO?" While He lived upon this earth, Jesus confessed on many occasions that He was in the world to do the will of God the Father. He was here to glorify God and finish the work God gave Him to do, and all hell could not stop Him until He could say, "It is finished!" Long before He went to Calvary, He looked His enemies in the face and declared, "He that sent me is with me: the Father hath not left me alone; *for I do always those things that please HIM*" (John 8:29).

We should follow in His steps. All that we do should be done to the glory of God. We should walk, talk, work, and witness to His glory. We should be very careful not to do anything that would bring reproach upon His holy name.

AS LORD OF THE HARVEST, HE WILL REAP

Writing to the Thessalonian believers, Paul said, "I would not have you to be ignorant, brethren, concerning them which are asleep, that ye sorrow not, even as others which have no hope. For if we believe that Jesus died and rose again, even so them also which sleep in Jesus will God bring with Him. For this we say unto you by the word of the Lord, that we which are alive and remain unto the coming of the Lord shall not prevent them which are asleep. For the Lord Himself shall descend from heaven with a shout, with the voice of the archangel, and with the trump of God: and the dead in Christ shall rise first: Then we which are alive and remain shall be caught up together with them in the clouds, to meet the Lord in the air: and so shall we ever be with the Lord. Wherefore comfort one another with these words" (I Thess. 4:13-18).

(Those of us who are saved are saved through the shed blood of Jesus; and if we depart this life before the Rapture, we will rest in Him as Saviour; but we will not be rewarded for our stewardship until the first resurrection.)

Notice in the passage just quoted, the word JESUS does not occur after verse 14. He is thereafter spoken of as LORD. *Jesus* died that we might be saved, and those who are saved (and who depart this life before the Rapture) *rest in Jesus* until the first resurrection.

Jesus came the first time to save sinners. He is coming the second time as LORD, and believers will be caught up in the clouds to meet Him. He is coming the second time to reward His servants for their faithful stewardship. We will reign with Him through the Millennium, and then throughout the endless ages of eternity.

After the Rapture, after the saints are taken, the Lord will judge the world. At the time of the flood, not one drop of rain fell until Noah and his family were safely in the ark and God had shut them in. No fire fell on Sodom and Gomorrah until Lot was safely outside the city. And the Church has His promise, *"Because thou hast kept the word of my patience, I also will keep thee from the hour of temptation, which shall come upon all the world, to try them that dwell upon the earth"* (Rev. 3:10).

We must remember that while Christ is Lord of the believer in a very special way, He is also LORD OF ALL. The world was made by Him, He was in the world and the world knew Him not — and the world does not know Him today. There is still "no room for Him in the inn." This world is being run by man — man's wisdom, man's religion, man's authority — *and man is receiving the glory.* But in spite of the fact that men are still saying, "We will not have this Man to reign over us," one day He WILL reign.

Yes, Jesus Christ will reign over this earth as Lord, and God the Father will see to it that He is universally acknowledged as God's Son. Every knee will bow and every tongue will confess that Christ is LORD, to the glory of God the Father. God decreed it, God said it — and His Word cannot be broken.

After the Church is taken out and all the saints are safe with the Lord in the air, a series of terrible judgments will fall upon this earth; and then after the Millennium the final judgment will fall upon mankind — upon those who have rejected the Saviour and refused the Lord of all things.

THE SECOND COMING OF CHRIST IN GLORY

God revealed this glorious event to John the Beloved on the Isle of Patmos, where He also revealed to him the horrible battle of Armageddon that will follow a thousand years later. Jesus will come in the Rapture and in the first resurrection. All the saints will be caught up to meet the Lord in the air. Then after the reign of Antichrist and the Millennium, we read:

"And I saw heaven opened, and behold a white horse; and He that sat upon Him was called Faithful and True, and in righteousness He doth judge and make war. His eyes were as a flame of fire, and on His head were many crowns; and He had a name written that no man knew, but He Himself. And He was clothed with a vesture dipped in blood: and His name is called The Word of God. And the armies which were in heaven followed Him upon white horses, clothed in fine linen, white and clean. And out of His mouth goeth a sharp sword, that with it He should smite the nations: and He shall rule them with a rod of iron; and He treadeth the winepress of the fierceness and wrath of Almighty God. And He hath on His vesture and on His thigh a name written, KING OF KINGS, AND LORD OF LORDS" (Rev. 19:11-16).

No one would deny that the Person riding the white horse is Jesus Christ. His name is Faithful and True, He is called The Word of God, He has eyes as a flame of fire, there are many crowns on His head and the armies of heaven follow Him on white horses. Out of His mouth "goeth a sharp sword," with which He will smite the nations — those nations who declared, "We will not have this Man to reign over us." But He WILL rule over them. He will tread the winepress of the fierceness of the wrath of God.

This Rider will have written on His vesture and on His thigh, "KING OF KINGS AND LORD OF LORDS." Certainly this could be none other than Jesus — He who died to save us, who rose from the dead and was exalted to the right hand of God the Father as *Christ the Lord*. He will return as KING OF KINGS AND LORD OF LORDS, and the horrible battle of Armageddon will be fought.

The Beast and the False Prophet will be cast into the lake of fire, the kings and mighty men who hated the Christ will be destroyed, Satan will be bound and put in the pit. Thrones will then be set, a Great White Throne will come into being, and all the dead will be judged. All the wicked will be cast into the lake of fire and there will be a new heaven, a new earth, and the Pearly White City. Jesus the Saviour who purchased the Church with His own blood and brought redemption to man and to all creation will then reign supremely in heaven, in earth, in the Pearly White City. He will then truly be LORD OF ALL.

The one thing that will determine whether or not you and I reign with Him is whether or not we receive Him as Saviour and surrender to Him as Lord of our lives. I John 2:28 tells us, "And now, little children, abide in Him; that, when He shall appear, we may have confidence, and not be ashamed before Him at His coming." Yes, there will be those who will be ashamed when Jesus comes — and there will be those who will not receive a full reward: "Look to yourselves, that we lose not those things which we have wrought, but that we receive a full reward" (II John 8).

Those who receive Jesus as Saviour and surrender to Him as Lord of their lives will be in that glorious number who receive "a full reward." Those who refuse to surrender to Him as Lord will suffer loss and be ashamed at His appearing.

In closing, let me ask you dear reader: Have you trusted Jesus as your Saviour? Is He YOUR Redeemer? Will you be one of those who receive a partial reward instead of your spiritual birthright — a FULL reward and the grand and glorious privilege of reigning with Him over all creation?

It is wonderful to know that we are saved, our sins are forgiven, and that we are redeemed by His precious blood — but have you recognized Him as your LORD and surrendered to Him? Is He truly Lord of your life. Are you just His son — or are you a son of God and a bondslave to the LORD?

He has a perfect right to everything you are and everything you have. If you are a born again believer and yet you refuse to surrender to Him and acknowledge Him as Lord of your life, you will be the loser and at the end of this pilgrim journey you will suffer — not the loss of your soul, but loss of your reward. If you have not surrendered to Him as Lord, do it now!

Believers should always look to Christ as our example. The first epistle of John is God's love letter to His "little children," and in that epistle we find the words, "AS HE" several times:

First, "If we walk in the light, AS HE is in the light, we have fellowship one with another, and the blood of Jesus Christ His Son cleanseth us from all sin" (I John 1:7).

In I John 2:6 we read, "He that saith he abideth in Him ought himself also so to walk, even AS HE walked."

I John 3:2: ". . . We know that when He shall appear, we shall be like Him; for we shall see Him AS HE is."

I John 3:3: "Every man that hath this hope in him purifieth himself, even AS HE is pure."

I John 3:7: ". . . He that doeth righteousness is righteous, even AS HE is righteous."

I John 3:23: ". . . Love one another, AS HE gave us commandment."

I John 4:17: "Herein is our love made perfect, that we may have boldness in the day of judgment: because AS HE is, so are we in this world."

This love letter which God dictated by the Holy Spirit to John the Beloved, penned down and sent to the children of God, closes with these words: "LITTLE CHILDREN, KEEP YOURSELVES FROM IDOLS." If there are idols in our lives, Jesus is not LORD of our lives; and if He IS Lord of our lives we will keep ourselves from idols.

May God help you and me to allow the Spirit to search our hearts and see if Jesus our Saviour is also LORD of our lives!

CHRIST OUR HOPE

CHRIST OUR HOPE

P AUL, AN APOSTLE OF JESUS CHRIST BY COMMANDMENT OF God our Saviour, and Lord Jesus Christ, which is our hope" (I Tim. 1:1).

This is the only place in the Scripture where we find the words, "Christ our hope," but even though the statement is not found, the *truth* of the statement is set forth in every book of the New Testament — and in some books it is set forth in every chapter.

Truly, Christ IS our hope. The Lord Jesus Christ is the object of faith for salvation to the sinner and the object of the life of faith to the believer. The Lord Jesus Christ is the HOPE of the believer as having to do with our eternal state.

In Acts 4:12 we read, "Neither is there salvation in any other: for there is none other name under heaven given among men, whereby we must be saved." In John 14:6 Jesus said, "I am the Way, the Truth, and the Life: No man cometh unto the Father, but by me." There is no other Name, there is no other Way. The Lord Jesus Christ *provided* salvation, and He is the object of faith *for* salvation.

In Galatians 2:20 Paul said, "I am crucified with Christ:

nevertheless I live; yet not I, but Christ liveth in me: and the life which I now live in the flesh I live by the faith of the Son of God, who loved me, and gave Himself for me."

For the believer, Christ is not only the object of our faith, but our faith is fed and sustained in Christ. We *live* by Christ, He is the life of our faith. Jesus said, "As the living Father hath sent me, and I live by (because of) the Father: so he that eateth me, even he shall live by (because of) me" (John 6:57). The believer lives by constantly appropriating Christ — that is, by receiving and feeding upon the Word.

"Now the just shall live by faith . . ." (Heb. 10:38).

"For the grace of God that bringeth salvation hath appeared to all men, TEACHING US that, denying ungodliness and worldly lusts, we should live soberly, righteously, and godly, in this present world; LOOKING FOR THAT BLESSED HOPE, and the glorious appearing of the great God and our Saviour Jesus Christ" (Tit. 2:11-13).

"Behold, what manner of love the Father hath bestowed upon us, that we should be called the sons of God: therefore the world knoweth us not, because it knew Him not. Beloved, *now* are we the sons of God, and it doth not yet appear what we shall be: but we know that, when He shall appear, we shall be like Him; for we shall see Him as He is" (I John 3:1-2).

"For we know that the whole creation groaneth and travaileth in pain together until now. *And not only they, but ourselves also,* which have the firstfruits of the Spirit, even we ourselves groan within ourselves, waiting for the adoption, to wit, *the redemption of our body.* For we are saved by hope: but hope that is seen is not hope: for what a man seeth, why doth he yet hope for? But if we hope for that we see not, then do we with patience wait for it" (Rom. 8:22-25).

In the Lord Jesus Christ we have salvation. In the Lord Jesus Christ we have life day by day as we trust Him — in Him we live and move and have our being. But our salvation does not end there. In Christ we have HOPE, and we look forward to that day when He will return, the time when we shall be like Him. Our salvation will then be *complete*.

Every child of God is looking for the blessed hope and longing for the glorious appearing of the great God and our Saviour, Jesus Christ. The grace of God that saves us also teaches us to look for our Saviour from heaven.

Jesus told His disciples that He would be arrested, tried, condemned and put to death. They were sad and heavy-hearted because of this announcement, but Jesus said, "Let not your heart be troubled: ye believe in God, believe also in me. In my Father's house are many mansions: if it were not so, I would have told you. I go to prepare a place for you. And if I go and prepare a place for you, I WILL COME AGAIN, and receive you unto myself; that where I am, there ye may be also" (John 14:1-3).

We are IN the world, but we are not OF the world. We are citizens of another world, strangers and pilgrims on earth as we await the return of our Lord. It is at His second coming that the born again believers shall receive the full fruits of redemption. It is when Jesus comes in the Rapture and the first resurrection that our vile bodies will be redeemed (Rom. 8:23). He will "change our vile body, that it may be fashioned like unto His glorious body, according to the working whereby He is able even to subdue all things unto Himself" (Phil. 3:21).

Thus the reason Paul declares *"we are saved by hope."* The Greek reads *"IN hope"* (Rom. 8:24). The soul is redeemed NOW (I Pet. 1:9); but we look forward to that glorious time *when our BODIES shall also be redeemed* from the power of death, delivered from suffering and from the grave. God has, in His grace, predestined us "to be conformed to the image of His Son, that He might be the firstborn among many brethren" (Rom. 8:29).

Even the *most spiritual* believers groan in this tabernacle of flesh. Regardless of how dedicated or fully surrendered to the Lord Jesus Christ one may be, ALL born again people will be called upon to suffer, to know sorrow, pain, and disappointment so long as we remain in these bodies of flesh. That is why all true believers are waiting for the coming of the Lord Jesus Christ. It is at His coming that we will receive complete and full deliverance from all that would hinder our enjoyment of the fullness of the salvation Jesus purchased on Calvary. As long as we remain in these mortal bodies we will be handicapped.

Saved ones who have departed this life are *resting in Paradise,* but they do not yet have the glorified body which they will receive in the first resurrection. They are resting, they are blessed — but they are not unconscious, the soul is not asleep. They possess some form of spiritual body but they will not receive a glorified body until the Rapture. At that time, *the dead in Christ will rise first,* then we which are alive and remain shall be changed and caught up together with them, to meet the Lord in the air.

Paul said, "If in this life only we have hope in Christ, we are of all men most miserable. But now is Christ risen from the dead, and become the firstfruits of them that slept. For since by man came death, by man came also the resurrection of the dead. For as in Adam all die, even so in Christ shall all be made alive. But every man in his own order. Christ the firstfruits; afterward they that are Christ's at His coming" (I Cor. 15:19-23).

THE HEART OF THE BELIEVER IS SET ON CHRIST

We wait and watch for the return of Christ our hope — not only because we will then receive our glorified bodies and be delivered from this vale of tears and disappointments, but also because *we long to see Him whom we love.* Christ is the object of our affections. We love Him because He first loved us — He loved us *long before* we loved Him. Since He loves us and we love Him, we are brought into fellowship with His love and His desires — and His desire is that we be with Him where He is.

In physical life, true lovers naturally desire the company of each other. Just so, Christ waits for that glorious moment when He will receive us up into the clouds to meet Him. Then will His heart be satisfied because those for whom He died will be with Him. In John 17:24 He prayed, "Father, *I will that they also, whom thou hast given me, be with me where I am;* that they may behold my glory, which thou hast given me: for thou lovedst me before the foundation of the world."

During His earthly ministry Jesus consistently taught His disciples of things to come, preparing them for His return to this earth. He exhorted them to watch and be ready for His return. In Matthew 24:46 He said, "Blessed is that servant, whom his lord when he cometh shall find so doing."

In Luke 12:35-38 Jesus said to His disciples, "Let your loins be girded about, and your lights burning; and ye yourselves like unto men that wait for their lord, when he will return from the wedding; that when he cometh and knocketh, they may open unto him immediately. Blessed are those servants, whom the Lord when He cometh shall find watching: Verily I say unto you, that He shall gird Himself, and make them to sit down to meat, and will come forth and serve them. And if He shall come in the second watch, or come in the third watch, and find them so, blessed are those servants."

In these glorious words the Lord Jesus Christ presents Himself to His disciples as the object of their faith while He is absent from them. Although He presents Himself to them as One departing, He makes it plain that His departure is in their interest: "*I go to prepare a place for you.*" And throughout eternity the redeemed will dwell in that place — the Pearly

White City, as described by John in the twenty-first chapter of The Revelation.

Jesus instructed His disciples that He was going away, He was going to prepare an eternal home for them, but He did not stop there. He further presented Himself as the object of their HOPE — He was going away, but HE WOULD RETURN; and when He returned He would receive them unto Himself, that they might be with Him in a world without end.

In I Thessalonians 1:9, 10 we read, ". . . Ye turned to God from idols to serve the living and true God; *and to wait for His Son from heaven,* whom He raised from the dead, even Jesus, which delivered us from the wrath to come."

Three things are clearly spelled out in these two verses:
1. The Believers at Thessalonica *heard the Gospel and turned to God from idols.*
2. They turned to God from idols *TO SERVE the living and the true God.*
3. *They WAITED for God's Son from heaven.*

Salvation brings life and service, and teaches us to look for the glorious return of Jesus. "So that ye come behind in no gift: *waiting for the coming of our Lord Jesus Christ*" (I Cor. 1:7). Paul wanted the believers in Corinth to have a full reward. He knew they were alive unto God, having received the Gospel and trusted Jesus as Saviour. He wanted them to be good stewards, not lagging behind in any gift of the Spirit but "waiting for the coming of our Lord Jesus Christ."

There is nothing that will so effectively cause believers to serve in sincerity and occupy faithfully until Jesus comes, as will the moment-by-moment expectancy of looking for His return. If we are *expecting* Jesus we will be busy FOR Jesus; and we will also be very careful where we go, what we do, how we live and how we use our time.

Paul said to the believers in Philippi, "For our conversation is in heaven; from whence also we look for the Saviour, the Lord Jesus Christ" (Phil. 3:20). According to the teaching of the epistles directed to the New Testament Church, we are definitely citizens of another world. Our citizenship is in heaven, our conversation is in heaven, our Head and Foundation is in heaven, and positionally we are already *seated with Christ* at the right hand of God the Father (Eph. 2:6; Col. 3:3; Heb. 1:1-3).

James admonishes, "Be patient therefore, brethren, unto the coming of the Lord. Behold, the husbandman waiteth for the precious fruit of the earth, and hath long patience for it, until he receive the early and latter rain" (James 5:7). We need patience. Most believers are prone to become *impatient*. We are prone to fret because of evildoers. We are tempted to be envious of the workers of iniquity. We look about us, and many times we see the *wicked* flourishing while the *righteous* suffer. But we are not to *look about* us; we are to look to JESUS and occupy until He comes. We are to pray for His soon return and live in expectancy of that blessed hope and that glorious event. Such living will cause us to be patient.

"Behold, I come quickly . . .

"And behold, I come quickly; and my reward is with me. . .

"He which testifieth these things saith, SURELY I COME QUICKLY" (Rev. 22:7, 12, 20).

The last declaration in the Word of God was made by Christ who said, "I go — I will come again." That declaration is, *"SURELY, I come quickly!"* And John the Beloved, to whom God dictated these words, said, *"Amen! Even so, COME, Lord Jesus."*

All dedicated, spiritually-minded believers can sincerely pray that prayer. If you cannot honestly pray, "Even so, come, Lord Jesus," there is something in your life that should not be there. We all have friends and loved ones who are dear to us, but it is Jesus whom we love most, and whom we desire to be with if we are what we should be as a child of God.

THE BIBLE BLUEPRINT OF THE RAPTURE AND THE FIRST RESURRECTION

The Apostle Paul was called and ordained a minister to the Gentiles: "For I speak to you Gentiles, inasmuch as I am the apostle of the Gentiles, I magnify mine office" (Rom. 11:13). It is not strange therefore that God should give to Paul His divine blueprint of the Rapture and the first resurrection. Paul was called, commissioned, and equipped of God to make known the Gospel of grace and the mystery of "Christ in you, the hope of glory" (Col. 1:27).

To the believers in Thessalonica Paul wrote, inspired of God, "But I would not have you to be ignorant, brethren, concerning them which are asleep, that ye sorrow not, even as others which have no hope. For if we believe that Jesus died and rose again, even so them also which sleep in Jesus will God bring with Him. For this we say unto you by the word of the Lord, that we which are alive and remain unto the coming of the Lord shall not prevent them which are asleep. For the Lord Himself shall descend from heaven with a shout, with the voice of the archangel, and with the trump of God: and the dead in Christ shall rise first; Then we which are alive and remain shall be caught up together with them in the clouds, to meet the Lord in the air: and so shall we ever be with the Lord. *Wherefore comfort one another with these words*" (I Thess. 4:13-18).

Here is what Paul clearly sets forth in these verses: —

1. There is no excuse for ignorance on the part of believers concerning the second coming of Christ and what will occur at that time.

2. There is no excuse for believers living in sorrow and sadness

concerning their saved loved ones who have departed this life, for we have *hope*. (Those who die without Christ *have* no hope.) From the Scriptures we can *learn* the estate and condition of our loved ones who have departed, and we know that our loved ones who are with Jesus He will bring with Him at His second coming.

3. We have the assurance that these are not the words of man. Paul says, "For this we say unto you *by the Word of the Lord.*" Therefore, these words are trustworthy and dependable. They are the Word of the Lord and they cannot be broken.

4. These verses give a clear outline of the things that will take place when Christ comes the second time:

(a) "The Lord Himself shall descend from heaven with a shout, with the voice of the archangel, and with the trump of God."

(b) "The dead in Christ shall rise first" — that is, all born again believers who have departed this life will be resurrected before anything happens among the living.

Nothing will happen among the living saints at the second coming until first the saints who have died are raised. We note in verse 14 that the Lord will bring the departed believers *with* Him. This refers to the spirit. When a believer dies the body returns to dust, but the spirit goes back to God who gave it (Eccl. 12:7). The Lord will descend from heaven with a shout, the dead in Christ will rise first, and the spirit will unite with the resurrection body.

THEN we (born again believers) who are alive "shall all be changed, in a moment, in the twinkling of an eye, at the last trump: for the trumpet shall sound, and the dead shall be raised incorruptible, and we shall be changed. For this corruptible must put on incorruption, and this mortal must put on immortality" (I Cor. 15:51-53).

(c) Then we which are alive and remain shall be caught

up *together with them* to meet the Lord in the air. Our loved ones who have died in the Lord will be raised incorruptible and the spirit will unite with the glorified body. Then we who are alive will be changed — this mortal will put on immortality. And together *all believers* will be caught up to meet the Lord.

(d) *"And so shall we ever be with the Lord."* Think of it! Never again to lose sight of His face! We do not see Him now except with the eye of faith; but we live in *hope* — the hope of His return.

We can say with Peter, "Blessed be the God and Father of our Lord Jesus Christ, which according to His abundant mercy hath begotten us again unto a lively hope by the resurrection of Jesus Christ from the dead, to an inheritance incorruptible, and undefiled, and that fadeth not away, reserved in heaven for you, who are kept by the power of God through faith unto salvation ready to be revealed in the last time.

"Wherein ye greatly rejoice, though now for a season, if need be, ye are in heaviness through manifold temptations: That the trial of your faith, being much more precious than of gold that perisheth, though it be tried with fire, might be found unto praise and honour and glory at the appearing of Jesus Christ: Whom having not seen, ye love; in whom, though now ye see Him not, yet believing, ye rejoice with joy unspeakable and full of glory: Receiving the end of your faith, even the salvation of your souls.

"Of which salvation the prophets have inquired and searched diligently, who prophesied of the grace that should come unto you: Searching what, or what manner of time the Spirit of Christ which was in them did signify, when it testified beforehand the sufferings of Christ, and the glory that should follow. Unto whom it was revealed, that not unto themselves, but unto us they did minister the things, which are now reported unto you by them that have preached the Gospel unto you with the Holy Ghost sent down from heaven; which things the angels desire to look into.

"Wherefore gird up the loins of your mind, be sober, and hope to the end for the grace that is to be brought unto you at the revelation of Jesus Christ" (I Pet. 1:3-13).

We have not seen Jesus with the natural eye, yet we love Him; and *believing,* we rejoice with joy so full of glory that it cannot be described in words. We rejoice because it has been revealed to us that we have an inheritance incorruptible and undefiled, an inheritance that cannot fade away, reserved in heaven for us.

We are kept by the power of God through faith, and we are "looking for that blessed hope and the glorious appearing of the great God and our Saviour, Jesus Christ." Through the inspired pen of the Apostle Paul, the Holy Spirit reveals to us the truth that was a *mystery* to the prophets (even when they prophesied) concerning *"the SUFFERINGS of Christ and the glory that should follow."*

The Old Testament saint could not understand the prophecies concerning the sufferings of the King of kings. They knew that He was to be *King of Glory,* but they could not understand the prophecy of the Lamb led to the slaughter, with no beauty that we should desire Him, smitten of God and afflicted (Isa. 53). But we who are on this side of Calvary understand clearly that the crown of thorns preceded the crown of glory, and that one day He *will come,* He *will be* King of kings and Lord of lords, and WE (the New Testament Church, His bride) will be with Him, never to be separated from Him again. "And so shall we ever be with the Lord."

(e) *"Wherefore comfort one another with these words."* In these days of sadness, heartaches, darkness and uncertainty, there is no message that brings such comfort and assurance to the heart of a believer as does that which declares the imminent return of the Lord Jesus for His Church. He may come — He *can* come— at any moment. There is nothing to hinder His coming. And "when Christ, who is our life, shall appear, then shall (we) also appear with Him in glory" (Col. 3:4).

THE RAPTURE AND THE REVELATION

There is much misunderstanding, even among believers, concerning the two phases of the second coming. First, the Lord Jesus will come *in the clouds in the air,* and the saints will be caught up into the clouds to meet Him. Then, after the marriage supper (at which time believers will be rewarded for their stewardship), *we will appear WITH Him in glory —* that is, we will be with Him in His glorious appearing, or, as the Greek reads, *"The appearing of His glory."* Thus, the saints will be with Him when He comes in the Revelation, when He is unveiled to all the earth and every eye shall see Him:

"Behold, He cometh with clouds and every eye shall see Him, and they also which pierced Him: and all kindreds of the earth shall wail because of Him . . . and lo, there was a great earthquake; and the sun became black as sackloth of hair, and the moon became as blood; and the stars of heaven fell unto the earth, even as a fig tree casteth her untimely figs, when she is shaken of a mighty wind. And the heaven departed as a scroll when it is rolled together; and every mountain and island were moved out of their places. And the kings of the earth, and the great men, and the rich men, and the chief captains, and the mighty men, and every bondman, and every free man, hid themselves in the dens and in the rocks of the mountains; and said to the mountains and rocks, Fall on us, and hide us from the face of Him that sitteth on the throne, and from the wrath of the Lamb: For the great day of His wrath is come; and who shall be able to stand?" (Rev. 1:7; 6:12-17).

The Lord Jesus will come *in the RAPTURE* to receive His own unto Himself; but in His *appearing* (the REVELA-TION), *the saints will come with Him,* and will reign with Him right here upon this earth.

Paul said to Timothy, "I give thee charge in the sight of God, who quickeneth all things, and before Christ Jesus, who before Pontius Pilate witnessed a good confession; that thou keep this commandment without spot, unrebukeable, *until THE APPEARING of our Lord Jesus Christ*" (I Tim. 6:13, 14).

The appearing of Christ is spoken of in connection with our responsibility in stewardship. *The earth* has been the scene of our service and stewardship, and therefore the earth will also be the place where our *reward* for faithful steward-ship *will be displayed.* Jesus said, ". . . Because thou hast been faithful in a very little, *have thou authority over ten cities*" (Luke 19:17).

In the first epistle to the believers at Thessalonica Paul unfolds the proper hope of the Church in the coming of Christ. He points out that they were not to be troubled about the believers who had already departed this life, neither were they to be troubled about their own position as relating to the Rapture of the Church. After he had unfolded this truth to them, he then speaks of their patience and faith in persecu-tions and tribulations that were coming upon them at that very time, and points them on to the time when they would have rest and deliverance from all of their trials:

"So that we ourselves glory in you in the churches of God for your patience and faith *in all your persecutions and tribulations that ye endure:* What is a manifest token of the righteous judgment of God, that ye may be counted worthy of the kingdom of God, for which *ye also suffer:* Seeing it is a righteous thing with God to recompense tribulation to them that trouble you; and to you who are troubled rest with us, *when the Lord Jesus shall be revealed from heaven with His mighty angels, in flaming fire taking vengeance on them that know not God, and that obey not the Gospel of our Lord Jesus Christ:* Who shall be punished with everlasting destruction from the presence of the Lord, and from the glory of His power; When He shall come to be glorified in His saints, and to be admired in all them that believe (because our testimony among you was believed) in that day. Wherefore also we pray always for you, that our God would count you worthy of this calling, and fulfil all the good pleasure of His goodness, and the work of faith with power: That the name of our Lord Jesus Christ may be glorified in you, and ye in Him, according to the grace of our God and the Lord Jesus Christ" (II Thess. 1:4-12).

The truth set forth here concerning the Lord's coming does not contradict the truth of the Rapture, but rather compliments the divine truth of the Lord's coming for His saints and the fact that the Rapture is the capstone of the pyramid of our hope.

Anyone who wants to know the truth of the second coming of the Lord Jesus Christ can find that truth clearly defined in the Word of God:

He will come first "as a thief in the night," to receive His jewels. *This is the Rapture of the Church* (I Thess. 5:1, 2; II Pet. 3:10).

Revelation 1:7 and 6:12-17 tell of the time *when every eye shall see Him.* This is the *Revelation.*

In the light of the Scriptures it is absolutely impossible to believe in *one coming,* and that when Jesus comes, all will be over in a moment, in the twinkling of an eye. The RAPTURE *will be over* in a moment, but in *the Revelation,* when every eye shall see Him, men will have time to pray! They will pray for the rocks and the mountains to fall on them and hide them "from the face of Him that sitteth on the throne," and from His wrath.

THE RAPTURE IS IMMINENT

The Rapture of the Church can (and may) happen at any moment. There is nothing pointed out in the Word of God as having to occur before the Rapture can take place.

Jesus taught that His coming for the saints was imminent. Between His resurrection and His ascension, Peter said to Him concerning John the beloved disciple. "Lord, and what shall this man do?" Jesus replied in these words: "If I will that he tarry till I come, *what is that to thee?* Follow thou me!" (John 21:21, 22). Had there necessarily been a long-drawn-out space of time between the ascension of Jesus and His return to this earth to catch away His saints, He could not have made this statement.

Paul believed in the imminent coming of Christ. He said to the believers in Corinth, "WE shall not all sleep, but WE shall all be changed. . ." The personal pronoun *"we"* included Paul along with the Corinthians. The same is true in I Thessalonians 4:13-18. Paul said, "WE who are alive and remain unto the coming of the Lord. . ."

According to the teaching of the inspired Word, there was nothing to hinder the return of the Lord during *Paul's* lifetime. Had Paul believed that there was a long course of time involved, a great number of years during which certain events must occur and certain earthly judgments must first be accomplished, he would never have included himself when he said "*WE* shall all be changed. . . *WE* who are alive. . ."

We are admonished, "Study to shew thyself approved unto God, a workman that needeth not to be ashamed, rightly dividing the word of truth" (II Tim. 2:15). But did you know that there are those who study and deliberately *wrongly* divide the Word in order to prove their religious points and their denominational beliefs? Some use the words of Jesus in attempting to prove that the Rapture is NOT imminent and that the second coming will be but one gigantic event when *all things* will occur simultaneously and be over in a matter of seconds. They use Matthew 24:29-31 to support their contention:

"Immediately after the tribulation of those days shall the sun be darkened, and the moon shall not give her light, and the stars shall fall from heaven, and the powers of the heavens shall be shaken: And then shall appear the sign of the Son of man in heaven: and then shall all the tribes of the earth mourn, and they shall see the Son of man coming in the clouds of heaven with power and great glory. And He shall send His angels with a great sound of a trumpet, and they shall gather together His elect from the four winds, from one end of heaven to the other."

Still others use these same verses to describe the Lord's return for the Church. The truth of the matter is that this passage from Matthew 24 *has nothing whatsoever to do with the Church.*

Paul said, "Give none offence, neither to the Jews, nor to the Gentiles, nor to the Church of God" (I Cor. 10:32). God is dealing with three groups:

1. *Israel* — whom we know today as the Jews.

2. *The Gentiles* — who had their beginning in the days of Nebuchadnezzar.

3. *The Church* — which was born on the Day of Pentecost and will be caught up in the Rapture to meet the Lord in the clouds in the air when Jesus comes to make up His jewels.

Matthew 24 has nothing to do with the Church, In the fifteenth verse of that chapter Jesus points out, "When ye therefore shall see the abomination of desolation, spoken of by Daniel the prophet, stand in the holy place, (whoso readeth, let him understand:) Then let them which be in Judaea flee into the mountains." We know that the *"abomination of desolation spoken of by Daniel the prophet"* will stand in the temple (which will be rebuilt in Jerusalem AFTER the Rapture). Therefore, *the Church is commanded to look*

for JESUS, not for "the abomination of desolation" which has
to do with *Israel,* God's ancient elect and chosen people.

In the same chapter, the Lord Jesus urges the Israelites
to pray that their flight "be not in the winter, neither on the
sabbath day" (v. 20). Certainly a true believer could never
pray this prayer, because the Sabbath was given to the
Jew. *Believers* worship on the first day of the week, the
Lord's Day, not the Jewish Sabbath.

In Matthew 24:23 Jesus warns, "If any man shall say unto
you, Lo, here is Christ, or there; believe it not." How could
this possibly be applied to the Church? How could the
Church be so deceived when *all believers KNOW* that Christ
is at the right hand of God? He is our Mediator with God
(Heb. 1:1-3; I Tim. 2:5). But the Jews are still looking for
their Messiah, and should one come to a Jew and declare, "Lo,
here is Christ . . . there is Christ," the Jew *could be* deceived,
because he is eagerly looking and praying for the coming of
Messiah, even to this very day.

The prophecy in Matthew 24 applies specifically to the
Jews, who at the time of the fulfillment of that prophecy will
be in Jerusalem and Judaea. Tens of thousands of Jews are already there and others are returning as rapidly as possible.

As further proof that this passage has nothing to do with
the Rapture of the Church, we read that after the tribulation
the sun will be darkened, and there will appear *the SIGN
of the Son of man in heaven.* They will see the Son of man
coming in glory. After this, He will send His angels with a
great trumpet to gather His elect. We know that such
prophecy could not refer to the Rapture of the Church. Believers who make up the New Testament Church are not looking for *signs* — we are looking for JESUS.

HIS APPEARING IN GLORY DESCRIBED

To John the Beloved, exiled to the Isle of Patmos for his
testimony, God revealed exactly what will happen when Jesus

returns to this earth with His saints. We find the record in Revelation 19:11-16:

"And I saw heaven opened, and behold a white horse; and He that sat upon Him was called Faithful and True, and in righteousness He doth judge and make war. His eyes were as a flame of fire, and on His head were many crowns; and He had a name written, that no man knew, but He Himself. And He was clothed with a vesture dipped in blood: and His name is called The Word of God. *And the armies which were in heaven followed Him upon white horses,* clothed in fine linen, white and clean. And out of His mouth goeth a sharp sword, that with it He should smite the nations: and He shall rule them with a rod of iron: and He treadeth the winepress of the fierceness and wrath of Almighty God. And He hath on His vesture and on His thigh a name written, KING OF KINGS, AND LORD OF LORDS!"

Here, spelled out in understandable language, is the description of the coming of the Lord Jesus Christ with His saints in judgment — the time when He will return WITH — not FOR — His saints:

"And the armies which were in heaven followed Him upon white horses, clothed in fine linen, white and clean" (v. 14). And *who are* these armies clothed in white linen? If we rightly divide the Word and compare spiritual things with spiritual, we need not wonder:

"Let us be glad and rejoice, and give honour to Him: *For the marriage of the Lamb is come, and His wife hath made herself ready. And to her was granted that she should be arrayed in fine linen, clean and white: for the fine linen is the righteousness of saints*" (Rev. 19:7, 8).

That is clear enough, is it not? The armies who followed Jesus in John's vision (the armies who will *literally* follow Him in His appearing) are the saints who make up the New Testament Church, *the bride of Christ.*

We must not confuse the coming of Jesus FOR His saints

and His appearing WITH His saints. He is coming in the Rapture to receive us unto Himself and reward us for our faithful stewardship; but He will appear in the Revelation to judge the world. It is clear, then, that the coming of Jesus for the Church will occur before He returns in judgment. I repeat — *there are not necessarily any intervening events between us and the imminent return of the Lord in the Rapture!*

HOW SHOULD THE NEARNESS OF HIS COMING AFFECT BELIEVERS?

Do we *really believe* that Jesus could come at any moment? Do we really expect Him moment by moment? Or do we live and act like the five foolish virgins of Matthew 25?

There were ten virgins. All ten went forth to meet the Bridegroom, all ten carried lamps, and while waiting for the Bridegroom all ten of them *slept.* At midnight there was a cry, "Behold, the Bridegroom cometh. Go ye out to meet Him!"

All ten of the virgins arose, all ten of them trimmed their lamps — and all ten attempted to LIGHT their lamps, but only FIVE would burn. The five foolish virgins who had no oil in their lamps had good intentions, they had the right desire, they *wanted* to see the Bridegroom; but instead of being alert, making sure that all was in order, they slept while they should have been watching — and sad beyond words, the five *wise* virgins slept when *they* should have remained awake; for had they been watching instead of sleeping, they could have warned the five foolish virgins when their lamps went out! They could have advised them where to buy oil (for since the foolish virgins *did* go for oil when they were so instructed, it stands to reason that they would have gone earlier had they been told to do so). The five wise virgins, even though they were prepared, they had oil in their vessels, and they went in to the marriage supper with the Bridegroom, *slept while their next door neighbors went to hell!* What a tragedy!

Are WE sleeping today, and allowing golden opportunities of stewardship and service to slip through our fingers? Is our light hidden under a bushel, or is it brightly displayed on a lampstand? Jesus said, "Ye are the light of the world. A city that is set on an hill cannot be hid. Neither do men light a candle, and put it under a bushel, but on a candlestick; and it giveth light unto all that are in the house. Let your light so shine before men, that they may see your good works, and glorify your Father which is in heaven" (Matt. 5:14-16).

Are we really "occupying" until His coming? Have we looked honestly on the fields that are white unto harvest? Do we see the multitudes scattered "as sheep without a shepherd"? If the imminent return of Jesus ever really grips our hearts, it will cause us to keep our lamps trimmed and burning. It will cause us to look on the fields that are white unto harvest — and do something about it. John declares, ". . . Every man that hath this hope in him purifieth himself, even as He is pure" (I John 3:3).

If we are what we should be as believers we will shine in a dark world. We will be beacon lights pointing men to Jesus: "For God, who commanded the light to shine out of darkness, hath shined in our hearts, to give the light of the knowledge of the glory of God in the face of Jesus Christ" (II Cor. 4:6).

To the Philippians Paul said, "Let your moderation be known unto all men. *The Lord is at hand.* Be careful for nothing; but in every thing by prayer and supplication with thanksgiving let your requests be made known unto God" (Phil. 4:5, 6). Believers should live and serve without a single anxiety to hinder, with our eyes fixed on the imminent coming of the Lord Jesus Christ. We should live, walk, and talk as if we expect Him at any second — and if we are spiritually minded, we DO expect Him at any moment. We do not know the time, we do not know the hour of His coming, but we do know that there is nothing to HINDER His coming this very day.

THEREFORE

"Be patient therefore, brethren, unto the coming of the Lord. Behold, the husbandman waiteth for the precious fruit of the earth, and hath long patience for it, until he receive the early and latter rain. Be ye also patient; stablish your hearts: for the coming of the Lord draweth nigh" (James 5:7, 8).

The hope of the soon return of the Lord is a perfect antidote for weariness, anxiety, trials, heartaches, and disappointments as we travel this wilderness journey — in a world of darkness, yet walking in the light; in a world of sadness — yet citizens of a land of gladness.

Jesus always emphasized the uncertainty of the time of His return, but he also urged His disciples to be alert. The hope of His coming is an incentive to fidelity. His command to the believer is *"Occupy till I come"* (Luke 19:13).

The second coming of Christ is *the hope of the Church.* His revelation and judgment of the wicked is the hope of *all creation.* When He comes in the final judgment, putting down the wicked and all wickedness forever, all things will then be made new. To ignore or deny the second coming of Jesus Christ is to close our eyes to one of the most powerful motives toward holiness and dedicated living to be found in all of the Bible. *"Every man that hath this hope in him purifieth himself."* Those who are looking for Jesus are careful how they live and how they conduct themselves.

The second coming of Jesus Christ is a vital part of Christianity, and any believer who refuses to study the Word of God concerning the second coming chooses to remain spiritually ignorant of his character as a believer and the place into which he is brought by faith in the finished work of Jesus.

Such a person is also ignorant of the fulness of the grace of God and the abundant life Jesus has promised.

Dear reader, are YOU looking for "that blessed hope" — the Rapture of the Church when Jesus will receive the saints unto Himself — both the living and the dead? Are YOU looking forward to that glorious appearing when we will reign with Him right here on this earth, when the curse will be lifted and all creation will be blessed, when the Millennial earth will be filled with the knowledge of the Lord as the waters now cover the sea?

Can you join John the Beloved in the last prayer recorded in the Word of God — "Even so, Come, Lord Jesus"? Would you rejoice to see Him today? Does it thrill your soul to face the Bible fact that He may come today, that we will see Him face to face, walk with Him, and be like Him? If you are saved by grace, if you have your lamp trimmed and burning, if you are a good steward in whatever duties the Lord has intrusted to you, the thought of the imminent return of Jesus will rejoice your heart.

If the second coming of Christ causes *fear* to grip your heart, the only wise thing for you to do is to fall upon your knees before God, and if you are not saved, ask Him to save you NOW. If you ARE saved but have not yielded completely to His blessed control, ask Him to cleanse you and make you meet for His use.

IN CLOSING

To sum up what we have covered in this message:

First, the second coming of the Lord Jesus Christ for His Church is the hope of the believer (I Tim. 1:1; Tit. 2:11-15).

The second coming of the Lord Jesus Christ is the hope of the entire creation which now groans and travails in pain, waiting for the redemption (Rom. 8:19-25; Isaiah 11).

The second coming of Christ is imminent — it can occur at any moment (Matt. 24:36; 25:13).

The second coming will be in two stages:

(1) Christ will come first (in the Rapture) FOR His saints (I Cor. 15:51-53; I Thess. 4:13-18). He will come as a thief in the night (I Thess. 5:2; II Pet. 3:10).

(2) After the marriage supper in the sky where believers will be rewarded for their stewardship, He will come (in the Revelation) and every eye shall see Him (Rev. 1:7; 6:12-17; 19:11ff.).

The second coming of Christ is *personal.* He is coming back personally, in a body, just as He promised the disciples (John 14:1-3; Acts 1:10, 11).

The second coming of Christ is Pre-Millennial. He will come to receive His own to be with Him in the clouds before He sets up the kingdom of righteousness here upon this earth. Before the kingdom can be set up, the King must return (Luke 19:12).

Until He comes the second time, Jesus has committed to us, His children, the "pound" of the Gospel with which we are to trade until His return (Luke 19:13).

The Lord's purpose in this day of grace is not to convert the world, but to gather out of the nations a people for His name (Acts 15:13-18).

Evil men and seducers will wax worse and worse. Evil will abound and *increase* under the rule of man and under the leadership of Satan, the god of this world (II Tim. 3:1-13).

The Lord Jesus Christ will come for His people and take them out of this world. He will raise the bodies of the born again dead and translate the living. All of this will occur before He comes with the saints to appear in judgment (I Thess. 4:13-18; II Thess. 1:4-12).

After the Church is taken out of the world, the Man of Sin will appear. He will sit in the temple and announce to the world that he is God. There will be a temporary peace.

Then in the middle of Daniel's seventieth week of prophecy the Man of Sin will break his covenant and all hell will be let loose upon earth. There will be a time of sorrow, suffering, bloodshed and misery such as has never been known, and unless the Lord should shorten those days there would be no flesh saved (Matt. 24:22).

Then after the destruction of the Man of Sin (II Thess. 2:8) Jesus will set up His kingdom of righteousness right here upon this earth and the Church will reign with Him for one thousand glorious years (Isa. 11; Rev. 20:4-6).

At the close of the Millennium we will enter into the eternal kingdom of God, and throughout the ages of ages we will rejoice in His presence.

For the believer, the best is yet to come! Therefore let us pray with John the Beloved, "EVEN SO, COME, LORD JESUS! AMEN!"